Becoming a Psychologist

Is psychology really the right career for you?

First edition

Edited by Dr Sokratis Dinos and
Dr Myrto Tsakopoulou

First edition 2012

ISBN 9781 4453 9729 0
e-ISBN 9781 4453 9738 2

British Library Cataloguing-in-Publication Data

A catalogue record for this book is available from the British Library

Published by

BPP Learning Media Ltd
BPP House, Aldine Place
London W12 8AA

www.bpp.com/health

Printed in the United Kingdom by

Ricoh
Ricoh House
Ullswater Crescent
Coulsdon
CR5 2HR

Your learning materials, published by BPP Learning Media Ltd, are printed on paper sourced from sustainable, managed forests.

BPP
LEARNING MEDIA

Contents

Free companion material		v
About the publisher		vi
About the editors		vi
About the contributors		vii
Shining a light on your future career path		ix
Introduction		x
1	How do you ensure psychology is the right career for you?	1
2	How to choose which psychology course and university to apply to	15
3	What steps are involved in the application process?	29
4	Life as a psychology student	41
5	Planning your finances	51
6	What does studying psychology involve?	63
7	What career paths are available with a psychology degree?	79
8	Becoming a clinical psychologist	95
9	Becoming a counselling psychologist	113
10	Becoming an occupational (or organisational) psychologist	127
11	Becoming a forensic psychologist	143

12   Becoming an educational psychologist   159

13   Becoming a research or academic psychologist 171

14   Conclusion   183

     Index   187

Free companion material

Readers can access additional companion material for free online.

To access companion material please visit:
www.bpp.com/freehealthresources.

About the publisher

BPP Learning Media is dedicated to supporting aspiring professionals with top quality learning material. BPP Learning Media's commitment to success is shown by our record of quality, innovation and market leadership in paper-based and e-learning materials. BPP Learning Media's study materials are written by professionally-qualified specialists who know from personal experience the importance of top quality materials for success.

About the editors

Dr Sokratis Dinos is a chartered psychologist with the British Psychological Society and is the Head of Psychology at BPP University College. He has worked as an academic psychologist for many years and has also been involved in the development of the Department of Health's mental health strategy. He has led the national evaluation of a number of mental health related programmes in the UK and has also worked as a research consultant for a number of independent organisations. His work has been published in a number of well-known academic journals.

Dr Myrto Tsakopoulou is a Chartered Counselling Psychologist working for the NHS and privately. She has obtained a BSc (Hons) Psychology, MSc in Health Psychology, MSc in Counselling Psychology and a Professional Doctorate in Counselling Psychology. She has worked extensively with people with mental health problems in a variety of settings such as prisons, rehabilitation centres, hospitals and community support services. She specialises in offering Cognitive Behavioural Therapy to individuals, couples and groups. She is a chartered counselling psychologist with the British Psychological Society, registered with the HCPC and is BABCP accredited.

About the contributors

Dr Marianne Rabassa CPsychol is a Chartered Counselling Psychologist. She obtained a Master's degree and Professional Doctorate in Counselling Psychology from the University of East London. She currently works for the NHS with a special interest in Cognitive Behavioural Therapy (CBT) and Psychosis, and in private practice in North London.

Katerina Kelesidi has worked exclusively in health and mental health academic research, conducting various clinical and longitudinal studies. She now uses her expertise in healthcare market research involving the management of global positioning, insight and communication studies. Katerina holds a BSc in Psychology from the University of York and an MSc in Mental Health from King's College London.

Dr Mark Flynn read English Language and Literature at Oxford University, before completing teacher training. He then taught English for several years in schools in Oxford and London, while completing a MA in Contemporary Literature and Theory at London University. He then turned to studying Psychology, following his Graduate Conversion with a Doctorate in Clinical Psychology at Royal Holloway and, more recently, a Postgraduate Diploma in Cognitive-behavioural Therapy for Psychosis at the Institute of Psychiatry. He has worked in Community Mental Health in east London for the last ten years and also practises privately.

Maria Tzortzaki MSc is a careers consultant who has worked across Greece and the UK providing career guidance and counselling to university students. She holds an MSc in Organisational and Social Psychology from the London School of Economics and in recent years has completed an MSc in Career Management and Counselling from the University of London. She is a member of the Graduate Careers Advisory Services and the Chartered Institute of Personnel and Development. She is currently working as a careers coach and is involved in designing undergraduate courses in Psychology.

Robert Goate MSc Occ Psych; Dip Couns; FCMI has worked as a business psychologist for twenty years, as Head of Development at media intelligence company Bradgroup, and as an independent consultant. He is also the editor of *OP Matters*, the journal for the BPS Division of Occupational Psychology.

Dr Gareth Norris is a lecturer in the Department of Law and Criminology at Aberystwyth University. He is a graduate of the MSc in Investigative Psychology at the University of Liverpool and completed his doctorate at Bond University in Australia. He specialises in studying the interaction between law, crime and psychology.

Dr Dimitra Pachi completed her BSc in Philosophy-Pedagogy-Psychology in the National Kapodistrian University of Athens, Greece before she moved to Surrey, where she completed her MSc in Social Psychology and then her PhD in social-developmental psychology. She is now a Lecturer in Developmental Psychology at BPP University College.

Dr Rumina Taylor is a Chartered member of the Division of Clinical Psychology (BPS) and a Practitioner Psychologist registered with the HCPC, UK. Rumina completed her clinical training at the Institute of Psychiatry, King's College London, before pursuing a joint research and clinical role at the Institute of Psychiatry and the Maudsley Hospital, South London and Maudsley NHS Foundation Trust.

Dr Emese Csipke completed her PhD in Clinical Psychology at the University of Manchester. She currently works at King's College London and is responsible for a large NIHR grant that aims to improve inpatient mental health services.

Shining a light on your future career path

The process of researching and identifying a career that you are most suited to can be a somewhat daunting process, but the rewards of following a career that truly engages you should not be underestimated. Deciding on your future career path should be viewed as a fun and extremely satisfying process that, if done correctly, will benefit you greatly.

Carefully considering a short list of future career options and what each one will offer you will help you to make a truly informed decision. Although it is perfectly acceptable to change career direction at a later date, reviewing the options open to you now will help to ensure that you are satisfied with your career from the outset.

I first began mentoring aspiring professionals eight years ago when it was clear that many individuals were not gaining access to the careers guidance they required. It was with this in mind that I embarked on publishing our *Becoming a* series of books, to provide help, support and clear insight into career choices. I hope that this book will help you to make an informed decision as to what career you are most suited to, your strengths and your aspirations.

I would like to take this opportunity to wish you the very best of luck with identifying your future career and hope that you pass on some of the gems of wisdom that you acquire along the way, to those who follow in your footsteps.

Matt Green

Series Editor – *Becoming a* series
Director of Professional Development
BPP University College of Professional Studies

Introduction

A career as a psychologist can be flexible, creative, interesting and rewarding but the training is long and demanding. This book is here to help you decide whether to take this professional path. To have a smooth progression through this path you will need to start making plans early. In this book you will find all the information you will need; from applying for undergraduate courses to doing postgraduate studies in a specialist field in psychology. This book will take you through all the necessary steps from the very beginning to becoming a practising psychologist in your chosen field.

First, you will need to decide if this is the right career for you. Chapter 1 will help you explore some important questions: do you have the skills, interests and qualities needed? Can psychology fulfil your needs and give you satisfaction as a profession? What challenges should you expect? Chapter 2 will give you some helpful advice on how to choose a course and university. Here you will need to consider a university course that will equip you with all the essential qualifications you will need in order to have a future career in psychology. Is the course accredited by the British Psychological Society? Does the university offer the appropriate facilities to make your student life a positive experience? Will it offer you the right skills and experience that you will need for the future? Chapter 3 gives you an overview of the application process. It includes information about how to apply and it offers many helpful tips from personal experience on how to prepare and apply.

Once you have made it to university a new life chapter begins. What is life like as a psychology student? In Chapter 4 you will learn about the course structure and available facilities found in the majority of UK universities. You will find tips and advice on how to 'survive' Freshers' week and how to make the most of your life as a psychology student. Recent changes in the educational law mean that tuition fees have had a sharp rise with massive financial implications on prospective university students. In Chapter 5 you will find an up-to-date overview of anticipated costs, including tuition fees and living expenses. It also offers some advice on how to save money as a student and what funding or other sources of income may be available to you. Chapter 6 includes an overview of the core psychology modules that your course will consist of.

Psychologists' careers are varied and there are different routes that get you there. A psychologist can work with children in schools, with offenders in prisons or in human resources. They may offer therapy to people in distress or they may carry out research in the community. These are all different career paths available to psychologists and how you will make use of your degree depends on your personal interests and skills. In Chapter 7 you will find an overview of the most established psychology career paths but also some information about other options available to you with a psychology degree. Many people who graduate with a psychology degree go on to work in a number of fields that may not be directly related to psychology.

The final six chapters will give you more specific details on six of the most popular and established careers in psychology: clinical, counselling, occupational, forensic, educational and research. There are a number of entry requirements in these specialist fields and most often you will need to have made the relevant provisions from very early on in your studies in order to maximise your chances of being accepted on these courses and subsequently go on to have a fulfilling career in your chosen field. In these chapters you will find all the information you need on the essential requirements of postgraduate degrees in these areas, how to apply, what the training involves and how to plan your finances. They also offer you some practical advice and some very useful tips from the personal experience of the authors that can help you along the way.

Chapter 1

How do you ensure psychology is the right career for you?

Dr Marianne Rabassa

Being a psychologist is a fascinating career that is both personally fulfilling and intellectually stimulating. It uses a scientific approach to understand people, the mind and behaviour. A psychologist can work in lots of different settings including the National Health Service (NHS), the prison service, schools, charities, universities or businesses. Although these roles may vary, what they will have in common is a commitment to continued professional development.

Often psychologists will be working with people who are experiencing difficulties in their life in some capacity. Working out how you can help people understand their problems, or perhaps feel less upset by what is going on, can be very rewarding. However, ensuring that you have the most up-to-date knowledge to best help each person involves an ongoing commitment to study and learning throughout your career.

Top tip

A psychologist will need to carry on updating their knowledge throughout their career. This may involve attending workshops, courses and ongoing reading.

Working as a psychologist can impact on your home life both while training and throughout your working life. This can be in positive ways; perhaps helping you communicate better with your friends and family. However, a negative aspect will be the reduced time you will inevitably have. For example, the average length of training to become fully qualified is seven years. Meeting the personal and academic requirements of the course of your choice is the first challenge. This will be followed by juggling academic work, your finances and gaining relevant work experience. It is likely that you will have less time and energy for friends and family than you have had in the past and romantic relationships could also be compromised. Therefore, before embarking on such a challenging but ultimately rewarding journey, it is vital that you consider carefully whether this is the right choice for you.

'Being on placement three days a week, attending university, completing course work and finding time to read important books and journal articles meant that friends saw less and less of me. It felt like I was completely absorbed in my training, and often took a while to return friends' phone calls. One friend in particular found this difficult to understand, and unfortunately now we don't really talk at all.'

What do you want from your career?

Before thinking about psychology specifically, it may be helpful to think about what you want from your career in general. Not everyone wants the same things or has the same priorities, so it's useful to be aware of what is important to you personally. Considering the following factors might help you.

Values

How do you define yourself and what is important to you? What would you like others to say about you and how you live your life? For example, is helping others something that is important to you? If so, how do you think you would like to do this?

When you've identified your priorities, it could be that other professions may be able to meet your values, in a less demanding way. For example, a youth worker, or support work can provide a valued helping role but do not require doctorate or master's level training. Equally, perhaps considering a medical based role such as a psychiatrist, or psychiatric nurse may fulfil your values better. Finding out more about these other roles will help you decide.

Money

Is earning lots of money important to you? Do you want your career to provide you with a certain standard of living, or to enable you to live in a certain style? A psychologist in the NHS starts on a wage of £25,000 per year while training and a rare few at the top of the profession can earn up to £97,000 per year. Not all psychologists work for the NHS however, and an average life-time wage is more likely to fall anywhere between £30,000 to £60,000 per year. There are also opportunities to set up independent practice and consultancy businesses, both of which can generate a healthy income.

Status

It may be that you would like your career to provide you with a certain status. Perhaps your parents or family would like you to have a professional career or maybe become a doctor. Many types of psychologists require doctoral level training to be fully qualified and many continue along an academic route to become professors. Developing a new theory or knowledge base can also result for a few in a renowned status. Many also become well known by commenting on issues in the media. However, although a large percentage of a psychologist's role is indeed sharing knowledge and theory, for most

this is achieved through discussing things with others, publishing research studies and consulting with other professionals rather than through public fame and fortune.

Personal development

You might be drawn to psychology through wanting to find out more about yourself. Perhaps you have been through some difficult past experiences and would like a career that would help you make sense of this. If this sounds relevant to you, it might be helpful to talk through these events and their impact on you with someone who knows you well in the first instance. Psychology is a demanding career, and it is important to work out if it is right for you. Talking through any personal issues, and knowing your own strengths and weaknesses is likely to help you become a more effective psychologist.

Top tip

Talking to a therapist or counsellor might help you work out if becoming a psychologist is the best way to resolve any personal issues.

'For me, being a psychologist reflects how I understand the world. I think that each individual has their own unique way of experiencing things. I love working with clients to try to understand things from their perspective and what might be the best solution for them. Often this can mean letting go of the idea that we have to get rid of someone's problem. It could be that learning how to accept things as they are is the most helpful approach.'

What are you good at / what do you find difficult?

For many people psychology is sometimes seen as a 'soft science' and an easy option to study over perhaps medicine or chemistry. However, for research psychologists in particular, analysing data will likely be a predominant part of their work. For other more clinical based roles too, science also plays a key role. Understanding an individual's distress or perhaps why they are not performing in their workplace, and then deciding what may be the best intervention will be based on existing research and theory, not just 'instinct'.

Top tip

Psychologists require a sound knowledge of how to analyse statistical data, conduct research and, in many cases, understand psychometric testing.

Psychologists need to be good communicators. This means having both good written and verbal skills. If you are involved in research, being able to pass on what you have discovered effectively to others is vital. Likewise if you are involved in clinical work you will also need to communicate with clients and other professionals. Being able to write about an individual sensitively and concisely can be a challenging task. Psychologists are often asked to provide an opinion or perspective that may not always be what people are expecting to hear. Communicating with others when they are perhaps angry or distressed involves patience and a willingness to consider others' points of views.

If you are someone that likes lots of physical activity throughout the day, then psychology may not be the best profession for you. For most branches of psychology, a large percentage of the psychologist's time will be spent sitting down, often in face-to-face contact with an individual. Being able to concentrate and retain large amounts of information is therefore also important.

Case study

'The first year of training was exciting and stressful in equal measures! It seemed like such a leap from learning the theory in lectures and workshops to then putting this into practice with real life clients. It often seemed like just as you were starting to understand a theory or concept, and feel a little bit more competent, you would start a new placement or start learning a new model and it felt like you'd just begun training again!

My placements included a children and families' service, an inpatient assessment unit and an older adult's therapy service. As well as learning different skills, there were also new colleagues to meet and locations to find your way around. On top of attending university and getting the coursework done it felt like you were constantly changing 'hats' which was very unsettling! Some placements were less enjoyable than others, some supervisors seemed more helpful than others and some work seemed to 'fit' better for me than others. In hindsight though, these less positive experiences were important

to clarify what you do want to specialise in and where you might or might not want to work.

By the third year, things started to come together a bit more for me. It felt less like I was 'pretending' to be a psychologist and I started to be more confident in my own strengths and what I could offer my clients. Having worked successfully now with a few people and seen them make genuine changes has been so rewarding and taking on board the feedback you get from supervisors and tutors certainly helped too.

Attending personal therapy during training is strongly encouraged and I know for me it certainly helped manage all the challenges and changes I was facing.'

Do you like routine or variety in your day?

As we have established, psychologists can work in very different settings and roles. An occupational psychologist for example might be helping an organisation work out how to increase staff satisfaction in the work place, while a forensic psychologist might be assessing the likelihood of someone re-offending. Psychologists may also be administering tests, planning and managing health services or writing up research at any one time.

Within each of these roles, there is the potential for establishing a regular routine to your week. For instance a psychologist in private practice may spend most of their time seeing clients face-to-face for an hour each from nine to five. If you like a little more variety, a working week could also include some time spent teaching at a college, while also working for a charity or support service on a different day.

If you prefer predictability however, psychology may not be the best career for you. Within each working day, there will be variety in the different types of people you will meet. Working with people can by its nature be unpredictable, and responding to crises, unexpected situations and highly expressed emotion means that one day can feel very different to the next.

'There is no such thing as a typical day. Last week, I spent three days doing clinic work. This included working with a refugee with post traumatic stress disorder and accompanying a young man with agoraphobia out to a shopping centre. I also attended a meeting with other professionals to work out a treatment plan for a client who is hearing voices. The next day I was teaching CBT skills at university, and then had a presentation to do at a conference for eating disorders. This meant also finding time to practise this on my colleagues!'

What are the most important things to you in your career?

Working out exactly what you want from your career as a psychologist will depend on what field you work in. Some broad areas to consider include the following.

Working conditions

Research psychologists very often work in academic settings such as universities so normal office hours might by the norm. However, gathering data, observing participants or administering tests or interviews might involve working more anti-social hours. Teaching is very often attached to such posts and may also involve working evenings and weekends.

Applied psychologists working in health settings or businesses usually follow traditional working hours, or perhaps the shift patterns of a hospital. Increasingly, psychologists also work in community settings and visit individuals at times and places that may be more convenient to them. This may therefore also involve working evenings and weekends.

Pay

Qualified psychologists working for the NHS or local authorities start on a pay scale of £30,000 to £40,000, with a senior level psychologist in a management post earning upwards of £90,000. However, earning a higher salary is generally related to levels of education, training and experience and therefore takes many years of working your way up through the ranks.

In the case of occupational psychology, the private sector tends to pay more than the public sector and although typical salaries might fall between £18,000 and £30,000, a private consultancy firm could

generate an income upwards of £80,000. However, it is likely that you will need a good knowledge of business and marketing to earn these higher sums. Although working in private practice can prove to be lucrative too, there is the necessity to remain competitive as well as the disadvantage of often chasing payments from clients and healthcare and insurance providers. Unlike the public sector a regular income at the end of each month is also not guaranteed.

Top tip

Generally, very few psychologists will reach the top ends of national pay scales and most earn a mid-range salary over the length of their career.

Autonomy

An advantage of working in traditional healthcare settings and particularly within private practice is the ability to set your own appointment times. Although if you prefer greater direction this may prove challenging, there is greater opportunity to create a work-life balance to suit you. If working in private practice, outside of meeting with a supervisor, the lack of opportunity to mix and discuss ideas with colleagues on a daily basis can also be isolating.

Do you have the right qualities to become a psychologist?

Due to the wide variety of different branches of psychology there is not one personality type that will be suited to all roles. For example, a research psychologist may benefit from a keen eye for detail and a good feel for statistics. An applied psychologist on the other hand may benefit more from good social skills and the ability to get on well with others. However, there are some qualities that could be beneficial across most fields. To help you work out whether these apply to you it can be helpful to ask those closest to you how they would describe you or what they think you are good at.

Patience

From the start of training and throughout their career, psychologists will be used to waiting for outcomes. From undergoing a lengthy training programme before becoming fully qualified, to the process of gathering enough data before you are able to analyse your results, patience will

serve you well. For those working in a clinical setting, working with a client who is not ready to make changes that you think may be helpful, will also need patience. Dealing with colleagues and other professionals with different views and perspectives can also be trying.

Critical thinking

It is helpful to be able to read research and listen to ideas with a 'critical' mind. In other words considering new information from all different perspectives and applying your existing knowledge to this new idea. Helpful questions that a psychologist will often ask include: what is this new idea trying to tell us? Can this be backed up by other ideas? What evidence is there? What more do we need to know?

Open-mindedness

Psychology is often about accepting that there is more than one way to understand events. Accepting that other opinions are also valid and finding ways to integrate this with what you already know will mean that very often we have to accept that there are no absolute truths. For some people tolerating this uncertainty can be a little unsettling.

Communication skills

Psychology is about the sharing of knowledge and ideas. This could be in meetings with other professionals, lecturing to a large group, discussing a topic on television, talking face-to-face to a client or publishing the results of your research. Being able to communicate both written and verbally concisely, clearly and confidently will help you 'sell' your ideas to others.

Empathy / listening skills

If you are thinking of becoming a psychologist it is possible you will have been told you are a good listener. Or perhaps you are someone that most of your friends come to with their problems. Being able to listen and problem-solve are definitely useful skills. However, for those working in a clinical setting, being able to listen to distressing and traumatic material on a regular basis can be at times upsetting and emotionally draining.

Top tip

It is important to accept that you can't help everyone. This means knowing where to place your own personal boundaries and what is 'too much' for you, as well as being aware that other services or professionals may be able to help someone better than you can.

So you still think psychology is the career for you? What next?

By reading this book you already have taken an important step in finding out more about a possible career. The next step is to find out as much as possible about the different branches to help you narrow your choices (see the following chapters for further information). You could look at the different job descriptions on the British Psychological Society website (www.bps.org.uk). You may even want to sign up for membership to this organisation. This would give you access to their monthly journal, *The Psychologist* This has articles about general psychological issues as well as job adverts for psychology graduates.

To help you find out if the job is right for you, you could try to contact registered psychologists to ask if they would be willing for you to shadow them for a day or perhaps meet with them for an informal chat. Although such requests are notoriously rarely granted (after all psychologists are busy people!), this has worked for some. You may also want to try this with other closely aligned professionals such as social workers or psychiatrists you might know to find out more about their roles. Contacting tutors on training courses to find out a bit more about the course requirements and what they would be looking for can also be helpful.

Overall, gaining experience in the following areas will be useful:

- Work experience / volunteering
- Research / assistant work
- Extra-curricular activity
- Counselling skills / workshops

Work experience

Gaining experience in your chosen psychology field will be difficult. However, any voluntary work involving contact with people would be helpful. This could be paid employment as a care assistant, youth worker, or nursing assistant. Particularly with applied psychology roles, getting used to being around people in a helping role would be useful. You could look for adverts for these posts in your local paper, or contacting charities directly.

Research / assistant posts

Research and assistant posts for graduates are notoriously difficult to obtain and therefore fiercely fought over. *The Psychologist* magazine may advertise these or the NHS job section online, or you could contact psychology departments directly to ask if they have any vacancies.

Extra-curricular activities

Being involved in groups or activities such as sports clubs, societies or charities will show employers and course tutors that you have the potential to achieve a good work-life balance as well as getting on with others. This might also give you the opportunity to practise your communication, organisational and leadership skills.

Counselling skills / workshops

If you want to work in clinical settings, achieving core training in counselling skills may help you decide whether this is the profession for you, as well as providing a welcome addition to your CV. There might be other skills that you think you need to build on. Short courses might help you do this. Workshops in topics such as research methods or support work may also be of interest to you. You can look at your local college prospectuses for what they have to offer.

Assess your skills

Ask yourself the following questions:

- Are you interested in studying and learning throughout your career?
- Are you prepared to make sacrifices to your home life?
- Does working as a psychologist match your own set of values?
- Are you prepared to earn a modest income?
- Have you talked through any personal issues with a therapist first?
- Do you have a good head for statistics?
- Do you have good communications and listening skills?
- Are you prepared for unpredictability, dealing with distress and uncertainty?

If you can answer yes to most of these questions then psychology might well be the career for you!

Chapter summary

Psychology is a varied field and one role can differ greatly from another. Finding out as much as possible about the different branches as well as thinking about what you want from a career is vital. Being a psychologist is rewarding professionally and personally but also involves commitment to ongoing study throughout your career. Before embarking on a long training path, it may be helpful to spend some time getting to know yourself, your interests and qualities before deciding if this is right for you. You might find that an alternative helping profession might suit you better.

Key points

- Get to know as much as you can about the different branches of psychology and what each role does.
- Think about what you want from a career.
- Think about what sort of person you are and what qualities you have. Does this match with the career you want?
- Could you build on your qualities with further studying or work experience?

Useful resources

Finding a therapist or a counsellor:
www.bacp.co.uk

Finding out more about psychology and roles:
The British Psychological Society: www.bps.org.uk

Finding out more about other roles:
NHS Careers: www.nhscareers.nhs.uk

Finding work and experience:
British Psychological Society appointments: www.psychapp.co.uk
NHS jobs: www.jobs.nhs.uk
Research academic jobs: www.jobs.ac.uk

Volunteering:
www.csv.org.uk
www.volunteering.org.uk
www.princes-trust.org.uk

Chapter 2

How to choose which psychology course and university to apply to

Katerina Kelesidi

Choosing a course can be very hard – it is a complex decision and this chapter is designed to help you identify the most important aspects that you need to look out for. These insightful tips will help you reflect on all the major factors in order to find the best fit between what you want and what a course can offer you. So, what are these? Let's begin!

Top tip

A psychology course offers the following.

- An understanding of the substance of psychology, with emphasis on the empirical study of mind, brain, and behaviour.

- A range of skills based on an understanding of the methods of scientific psychology, including hypothesis testing, information-handling, and the critical evaluation of empirical data.

- A range of more general skills in problem-solving and effective communication, so as to facilitate access to a broad range of educational and employment opportunities after graduation.

Accreditation

The British Psychological Society (BPS) is the representative body for psychology and psychologists in the UK. The BPS is responsible for the development, promotion and application of psychology. It is also the body that ensures that the education of psychology is of the required standard. The BPS accredits those courses where the educational programme is in line with that of the development and application of psychology. As the BPS states:

> 'accreditation is how we reach a view on whether psychology courses are suitable to support students' achievement of learning outcomes, and are supported by an appropriate resource base. It is how we engage in dialogue with providers of psychology education and training, and providing a detailed external review of each course' (BPS, 2012).

It is important to remember that not all university courses are accredited by the BPS. This can be a very important factor that will help you to decide which course to choose.

After successful completion of your accredited undergraduate psychology programme you will be eligible for Graduate Membership of the BPS and have the Graduate Basis for Chartered Membership (GBC), provided the minimum standard of a lower second class

honours is achieved. This is the first step towards becoming a chartered psychologist as GBC is a pre-requisite for a number of postgraduate courses in psychology that provide training in specialist fields in psychology (eg Doctorate in Clinical Psychology, Doctorate in Counselling Psychology, MSc in Forensic Psychology, MSc in Occupational Psychology, MSc in Health Psychology). Chartership is also an essential requirement of many employers (for example the NHS). So if you want to pursue a career in any branch of professional psychology it is advisable to choose a BPS accredited undergraduate degree course. It also allows you to register with the society for a lower fee than other membership levels which will give you online and print access to new developments and specialised careers within psychology.

Top tip

If you are considering a career in psychology, you should choose a course with the following two aims in mind.

- BPS Chartership: Chartered psychologist status is the benchmark of professional recognition for psychologists; it reflects high standards of training and expertise. It is also a requirement by many employers. Look out for BPS accredited courses which can offer you eligibility towards Graduate Basis for Chartered Status (GBC).

- HCPC registration: the Health and Care Professions Council (HCPC) is a regulatory body which was set up to protect the public by keeping a register of health professionals who meet certain standards. If you wish to practise psychology under one of their protected titles (eg counselling psychologist or educational psychologist) you will need to be registered with the HCPC. The majority of courses accredited by the HCPC also require GBC. Check the Useful resources section at the end of the chapter for the HCPC website.

However, if you decide to go for a course that does not yet have a BPS accreditation, there are a number of conversion courses that you can undertake (once you have successfully completed your degree), and they can be found on the BPS website. Chapters 3 and 6 give you more information about accredited and conversion courses in terms of content and requirements.

> 'When I first started, I was nervous and a bit anxious about how university life would be, but I was lucky to have met so many people from my course who were all really friendly. I have thoroughly loved my first year of studying psychology; I have learnt a lot of interesting theories and have participated in experiments. The lecturers have been really supportive and approachable, which makes the course a real treat. They have always been happy to help and it gave me a lot of confidence.' **Anna, Year 2 Psychology student**

Module factors

Compulsory modules

One of the important elements for choosing a psychology course is the variety of offered modules – both compulsory and optional. All the BPS accredited courses contain some core modules that consist of the well-established psychology modules such as developmental, social, abnormal and cognitive psychology. Statistics, using a specialist package (usually SPSS) is also a mandatory module that advances with the year you are in. Compulsory or standard modules that the majority of courses include are described in Chapter 6.

Elective modules

Most universities offer a variety of optional modules that relate to a number of specialist fields in psychology such as neuroscience, health psychology, organisational psychology and forensic psychology to name a few and these are typically offered in the final year of your studies. However, the range of choices may by degree types; for instance graduate diploma courses have a smaller range of elective modules. Such modules can be chosen while studying for your compulsory modules. Some courses may offer additional elective modules from other disciplines, which you can study along with your psychology modules. Popular choices include modules from sociology, history and philosophy.

Course direction

Another aspect that you should look out for is the overall direction of a course. For example, some universities are primarily focused on the experimental-research side of psychology and some others are primarily committed to the clinical side of psychology. Since it is hard to know which 'side' of psychology you will be most interested in at this

stage, a university course that offers an equal grounding of different specialist fields is the safest bet. Different specialist fields in psychology are extremely useful for your own learning and understanding of psychology but also for your future employability.

'One of the reasons I chose the course I did was because it offered a great variety of modules and the advantage of a Year 3 placement in a highly regarded educational setting. This experience gave me a great insight of how it is to work in academic research. I had the opportunity to apply and develop my research skills and collaborate with the institution for my third year project. Invaluable!'
Shelley, Year 2 Psychology student

Type of course

Nowadays, an increasing number of universities offer more than one type of psychology course. Currently, there are three types of psychology course: single honours, joint honours and sandwich courses. Table 2.1 presents an overview of the advantages and disadvantages of each type of course.

In England and Wales, typically all undergraduate honours degrees last three years and consist of 360 credits – 120 for each year. In Scotland all undergraduate degrees last four years.

Single honours course

Doing a single honours psychology degree is the most popular choice and all universities offer this choice. Doing a single-honours psychology degree means that the majority of your modules will be part of the psychology curriculum. They can be either BSc or BA but you need to ensure that they are BPS accredited. There are some accredited BA courses but in some cases you may need a conversion diploma to obtain BPS accreditation.

Joint honours course

Taking a joint honours degree means that you devote 50% of your time studying psychology and the other 50% on a different subject. Typically, in all years you will have to cover the core psychology modules – on both basic and advanced level (more details on these can be found in Chapter 6). Advanced statistics and research methods are an absolute prerequisite for obtaining a psychology honours degree. The other subject can be anything you choose, although most

universities will offer a list of subjects that you can undertake when you study psychology. For instance, some popular subjects paired with psychology are: computing sciences, history, management studies, marketing, philosophy, sociology, physiology, law, criminology and many more. As you can see, there is an exciting range of subjects that can give you an amazing advantage of connecting psychological principles to other subjects.

But are there any disadvantages? As everything in life comes with advantages and disadvantages, so does such a decision. It can be very rewarding to be able to study two subjects that are of interest to you but the trade-off might be the lack of specialised knowledge in an area of psychology, such as advanced cognitive psychology. Another disadvantage can also be the BPS accreditation as not all universities that offer a combined degree have BPS accreditation.

The truth is that no matter whether you study for a single or joint honours degree you will be expected to work hard; it is certainly true that the effort you put in is rewarded by the standard of the degree you graduate with.

Sandwich courses

Sandwich courses are four-year courses, and are increasingly popular. They offer a placement in Year 3 with an opportunity to specialise in the final year. Most universities that offer sandwich courses have professional schemes with institutions and companies that have psychology-related areas of work.

Professional placements can be really insightful; they give you the opportunity to spend part of your degree programme with an outside organisation, gaining invaluable work experience and enhancing employability.

Single honours	Joint honours	Sandwich
✗ Not being able to study other interesting subjects	✗ Lack of specialised psychology knowledge	✗ Four years
✓ In depth knowledge of psychology	✓ One more interesting subject under your belt	✓ Work experience
✓ BPS accreditation	✗ BPS accreditation	✓ BPS accreditation

Table 2.1: Advantages and disadvantages of each type of course

Ranking and reputation

Since studying psychology requires a lot of focus, determination and money commitment, choosing a course in a university that has a good enough ranking is a good idea. Every year respectable newspapers publish a comprehensive list of all UK universities. These include rankings by subject which are much more informative than overall rankings. These can also be found online along with other similar sites – see Useful resources at the end of the chapter.

There are a couple of pieces of advice you should be aware of in order to be able to make a decision that fits your expectations. Student satisfaction and graduate prospects ratings are the two key factors that you should always look out for on a ranking table. These will be indicative of how satisfied students were with the course and the proportion of the students that were employed once they graduated. Course satisfaction and employability are both important factors you will need to consider before you decide which university to apply for.

Employability

As markets become increasingly competitive, employability should be carefully considered. Employability is a combination of factors which enable people to get into employment, to stay in employment, and to move on in the workplace. A good indicator of employability is the number of students that have gained employment after they have graduated. General information about employment is often found on university websites and / or their brochures, but also on the league tables of established newspapers or on the Universities and Colleges Admissions Service (UCAS) website. If you attend any open days,

BPP
LEARNING MEDIA

make sure you ask for more information so as to get a better idea about the type of industries their graduates get employed in. In times when competition for employment is tough, such information can be particularly insightful in helping you to decide where to study.

Top tip

A good way to find out more about potential psychology courses is to attend university open days: you will be able to meet current students, graduates and course leaders or lecturers who can give you invaluable information towards making the right decision.

Fees

Given the new rise in the student fees, the financial factor is a great one and cannot be overlooked. Some universities have already announced that they will charge the top level of fees whereas others will be offering a more economic option.

Students in the UK but also in Scotland, Wales, and Northern Ireland are eligible for a means-tested grant offered by the government. European students are also eligible but Non-European Union students are not subsidised by the UK government and so have to pay much higher tuition fees.

Further, most universities in the UK have a range of studentships and bursaries that are given to bright students that have low financial capacity. More information about such options can be found in the psychology course details of each university. You can also find more details on fees and how to plan your finances in Chapter 5 of this book.

Location and accommodation

In England and Wales the majority of young full-time students attend universities situated a long distance from their family homes. For this reason most universities in the United Kingdom will provide rented accommodation for many of their students. University accommodation (such as halls of residence) is usually available for all Year 1 undergraduate students whereas Year 2 and 3 students tend to rent privately with friends.

Nevertheless, some universities may be able to provide accommodation for the full duration of the course. Because of the recent rise in fees, an increasing number of students choose to go to universities located

close to their family home. In that way, any additional costs can be minimised.

However, beyond the financial reasons, university location can be indicative of a student's lifestyle. Universities located outside of big cities or towns are usually campus-based. The campus location means that all departments and offices, but also all events and courses, are taking place within campus which makes a huge difference to student lifestyle. It is particularly attractive for Year 1 students as it makes academic and social settling down much easier. From getting to your lecture stress-free to socialising without worrying about transport, it can often be a huge contributor to a good undergraduate lifestyle.

On the same token, a university located in a big city can offer a much wider variety of entertainment and educational opportunities – from museums and theatres to a range of free lectures. Nevertheless, the cost as well as the practicalities of living in a big city should not be underestimated. Travelling to and from places can be a significant part of your daily routine. Also low rent student accommodation can often be very limited. More information about the costs and different types of university accommodation can be found on universities' websites. However, it's worth visiting a comprehensive site on the different types of student accommodation, inclusive of university accommodation, (see Useful resources).

Something for mature students

Learning throughout the lifespan is what defines our era. Students come from all walks of and from every stage of life. Mature students decide to study for many different reasons, including improved job prospects, making a fresh start or purely for interest in their subject.

Mature students comprise the vast majority of part-time students and a large proportion of the full-time student population across the UK. They bring the experience and the wisdom that enables a good debate and an excellent mix of people necessary for producing a successful psychology year!

Universities and colleges welcome mature students and value them not just for their enthusiasm, but also for their experience and skills. Course admission requirements reflect that and their range of qualifications are often considered. A large number of universities and colleges also provide a selection of flexible learning programmes, such as evening lectures and weekends. The equal opportunities law also ensures that employers cannot discriminate on the basis of age and, for most positions, age limits are no longer appropriate.

Case study

'I left school at age 16, straight after my GCSEs without any career aspirations – all I wanted was to find a job and start living like an adult. When I started thinking about studying, I spent some time on individual university websites initially. I started a one-year course at the beginning just to test how I would do; I did not think at that point about going back to full-time education! However, I loved the subject and the learning process so much that my learning overtook my work. So, I decided to become a full-time student and do a three-year degree. As you can imagine, my lifestyle changed completely – I had always lived in the same town and suddenly I had to go and meet a whole new city and new people! I came to Portsmouth with my husband and at first the thought of relocating was terrifying, both in terms of finance and practicalities. Despite all these, I managed to study full-time by working part-time throughout my degree. I met some great people and found my subject fulfilling; the academic staff have been extremely understanding and approachable'.

Chapter summary

Choosing a course has several parameters that should be taken into account in order to make a decision that meets your expectations. Content of modules, BPS accreditation, university reputation, location, employability and type of degree are some of the factors that you need to think about and research before your studies. This chapter has provided you with an overview of all the different elements that need to be weighted for making the best possible decision and ensuring you have a great learning of psychology and a great living!

Key points

Choosing the right course and university is an important decision to make which will define the quality of your studying experience and your future employability. Some questions to consider when choosing include:

- Do you wish to pursue a future career in professional psychology? If yes, is the course accredited by the BPS and will it lead to eligibility for GBC?

- Do the course modules look interesting and will they give you knowledge in the specific psychology field you are interested in?

- Is the ranking and reputation of the university and the psychology department important to you? Do you think these factors may be significant in your future career?

- If you have a special interest in a specific area of psychology, either professionally or for research, does the course offer good prospects in this field? For example, is research in this field being carried out there? Or are there lecturers with published work in this area?

- Are practical factors, like fees, accommodation options and proximity to home more important for you?

Useful resources

University ranking tables:
www.guardian.co.uk/education
www.thecompleteuniversityguide.co.uk/league-tables

Information about psychology accredited courses, professional specialities: www.bps.org.uk/careers-education-training

Health and Care Professions Council:
www.hcpc-uk.org

Information about how to choose a course (entry requirements etc):
www.ucas.com/students/choosingcourses

Oxford University entrance requirements:
www.ox.ac.uk/admissions

University of Cambridge entrance requirements:
www.cam.ac.uk/admissions

Info about student accommodation:
www.studentpad.co.uk

Info about how to manage your finances:
www.studentfinance.direct.gov.uk

Reference

British Psychological Society (2012) *What is Accreditation?* [Online] Available at www.bps.org.uk/careers-education-training/accredited-courses-training-programmes/what accreditation/what-accreditat [Accessed 25 June 2012].

Chapter 3

What steps are involved in the application process?

Dr Mark Flynn

This chapter gives an outline of the main steps involved in applying to study, or *read*, as it's sometimes termed, a psychology degree at university and to offer some personal tips and reflections that, as well as instructing, will help to bring the application process to life.

Top tips

- While information presented here is up to date at the time of writing, always check with specific universities and other relevant professional bodies for the very latest information on applications.

- Just some of the useful, online, sources of information available include the British Psychological Society (BPS) website and the website for the Universities and Colleges Admissions Service (UCAS), whose form you'll complete when applying.

So, you've arrived at the position that you think you want to embark on a psychology degree. Congratulations! Whether you're in your late teens and at school or college, or in your 20s or older, and working, you are on the brink of a making a decision that will not only influence your immediate learning opportunities, possible future training and your consequent career path, but also radically alter fundamental ways in which you think about yourself and others.

Routes to studying for a psychology degree

There are two main routes by which you might finally come to study psychology at university:

1. As an undergraduate, most likely closely following completion of A levels and because of a mainly academic interest, or

2. As a graduate, most likely entering onto a conversion diploma for graduates after employment and an undergraduate qualification in a different field, and because life experiences have reconfigured your perspectives to make you want to learn more about the human condition.

Whichever route you take there will be fierce competition for places: there has been a steep rise in the number of people applying to study psychology, at every level at university, in recent years. So you'll need to have good academic and other personal credentials, and great determination.

If you are taking the first, undergraduate route, you are likely to be completing your A levels, and struggling to stay sane as you also

contemplate the UCAS form. Or you may be applying post A levels after a relatively brief period of employment or gap year.

If you are applying via the second route, as a graduate, then you'll be older; you may have found some unsatisfying limits to your current employment and have doubts about the utility of the qualification(s) you've attained, at least insofar as where you now want to be heading is concerned. Perhaps you have begun to realise that if you'd known more about what psychology encompasses when you were making previous decisions about your academic career you'd have chosen to pursue it then, over English, Maths, French, Business and IT – whatever you studied previously.

The undergraduate route

Different courses will have different requirements, but prospective psychology undergraduates should bear in mind that they will need two A levels and four GCSEs grade A–C (including English and Maths) as a *minimum*. If you have an A level in Maths or another science then many institutions will look favourably on your application. Having A or AS level Psychology is not normally essential, but it may place you at an advantage when applying and when beginning studying.

The conversion route

If you are a graduate applying to read psychology, then unless you are going to study the subject purely out of interest you are probably making a significant change of direction and entering the field with a view to making a career of it. That is, your degree will be just the first step of a long journey and you'll be hoping to do further specialist study after you've completed this first stage.

This is where conversion courses come in. Rightly or wrongly, most graduate conversion diplomas in psychology assume that you already have some relevant transferable knowledge and learning skills; accordingly, such courses allow you to forego engaging with several less essential modules that undergraduates complete as a part of the degree and to concentrate instead on the essentials and some personal options. Most conversion courses can be studied either full-time over a very intensive 18-month period, or part-time over approximately three or four years, or 'mixed-mode' (a combination of full-time and part-time, lasting between 18 months and four years, as suits).

Top tip

The core modules of a conversion psychology course are:

- Biological psychology
- Cognitive psychology
- Developmental psychology
- Individual differences
- Social psychology
- Conceptual and historical issues in psychology
- Research methods

While conversion courses vary, most will require that a graduate has GCSEs including Maths and English, possibly a science among your A levels, and a good degree (which usually means a minimum of a 2:1). Check such details with course prospectuses / admissions tutors and whether or not the courses you are applying to are BPS accredited and confer GBC status, an essential requirement for entry onto accredited postgraduate training courses and chartered psychologist status. You can also find more information about conversion courses in Chapter 6 of this book.

Case study: A personal experience – statistics!

'If my experience and that of many colleagues is to be put to good use, it seems important to acknowledge a subject many will perceive only as a word looming in blood-soaked gothic script and trailed by a comet of stabbing exclamation marks, namely: statistics!!!!! Tutors will confirm that anxious queries about this standard component are among the most frequently asked questions (FAQ) they routinely deal with: how much maths is there on the course? How difficult is the statistics component? What if I'm useless at maths?

If you've followed your Maths GCSE with an A level in Maths, you won't be worried about confronting and interpreting numerical data – indeed, you may relish the prospect. However, the wide intake onto psychology degrees means that many entrants have little or no familiarity with working with numbers beyond what they can recall, with a shudder, of their Maths GCSE. So, let's be clear: you will be working with numerical data – a lot of it. But calm yourselves; my own experience should help.

Speaking as someone who failed his Maths A level after drawing a fairy sitting atop a mushroom because he couldn't answer a single subsection of any one question, and who later in life managed to complete a graduate conversion diploma in psychology, followed by a doctorate in clinical psychology and then a postgraduate diploma in a further specialist area – I can safely say that fears about numbers are conquerable. Most courses are well aware of the difficulties that the statistics, or research methods, components present to those from an arts and humanities background. While research methods modules will always provide a considerable challenge for mathematics muppets like me, most courses make efforts to factor in students' unfamiliarity with and insecurity about these modules and teach them thoughtfully and supportively, providing supplementary teaching for the numerically challenged.

If you're a graduate converting to psychology from an arts and humanities background, unless you are with good reason especially confident I'd strongly recommend that you think very carefully before embarking on a full-time conversion: as discussed above, the statistics and research methods modules of psychology can be daunting initially, and will require a different way of thinking and writing than you've been used to. You'll need time in which to adjust to this new way of learning and developing the skills required for completing research-based components of the course. Adjusting to processing this new kind of information while also managing the considerable burden of other, albeit perhaps familiarly discursive, course modules will bring pressures and might compromise your chances of overall success. I and several peers from similar, non-science, backgrounds definitely benefited by doing the conversion via a 'mixed-mode' approach.'

Top tips

- Preferably pursue a course that's accredited by the BPS and confers eligibility for Graduate Basis for Chartered Membership (GBC), which you'll need if you want to do postgraduate studies with a view to becoming a chartered psychologist.

- If you're doing a modular, joint or combined honours course, then you'll need to check with course tutors which modules in what combination will guarantee accreditation.

- If you're a graduate converting from the arts and humanities, think carefully about giving yourself sufficient time in which to manage the research methods modules and choose your mode of study (full-time, part-time, or mixed mode) accordingly.

Application forms

This chapter will not provide details of the UCAS process or any other specific supplementary forms that some courses might require of you. Application processes can change, and schools, colleges, UCAS itself, and university admissions departments are best placed to supply you with up-to-date information on what the relevant forms are, how to access them and the steps you need to take to complete your application properly (consult the UCAS website cited at the end of this chapter).

What *is* worth commenting on is *how* you complete your application form. Put simply, your application form is the only knowledge of you that a course will have prior to deciding whether or not to invite you for interview and / or offer you a place. Given that, it is essential that your application form is completed correctly and impressively. Individuals who complete forms incorrectly and sloppily will, clearly, be at a disadvantage compared to those who have put in the due time and effort and presented forms accurately, with some evident consideration of content and style. It is important, therefore, to draft your application several times, gradually building up relevant content, layer by layer, before editing features such as spelling, punctuation and grammar. When you have had several weeks / months to prepare before sending off an application – time enough in which to work on it, finesse it and have others cast a constructively critical eye over it for you – it should be pretty much flawless. Certainly, sections relating to personal details and academic achievements should be absolutely error free – after all, their completion is merely an exercise in accurately relating the facts as they stand. Those sections inviting more subjective, discursive reflections, including your reasons for applying for psychology and your other interests and achievements, are clearly more challenging and ideally should be characterised by a sense of interest and enthusiasm, confidence tempered by modesty, and an absence of high-sounding, but often utterly meaningless, jargon and cliché.

Whether the tutor responsible for assessing your application form is reading it at 3.15am while simultaneously trying to ignore their newborn's wailings, or doing so at 8.15am, having cut short their morning run round the local park, is a matter of importance. The individuals assessing your forms are human and have lives. Regardless of what universities might seek to suggest both to prospective students and to their own employees about the application and assessment process, the grim reality is that few if any tutors are provided with a comfortably-cushioned space and endless time in which to assess your form, muse on those possible virtues that you have unfortunately failed to convey and give you the benefit of the doubt. Whoever is assessing

your application form is very likely to be doing so in their personal time; it goes without saying that they are not going to be happy about that and their threshold for getting irritated is going to be lower than usual. So, put simply – and, thinking psychologically – don't annoy them further by writing in a sloppy or a needlessly dense, complicated fashion. If you do then your application will, quite simply, be rejected.

Experience

Admissions tutors will understand the likely limited life experience of individuals in their late teens applying for undergraduate courses; still, if you have already gained some relevant experience or knowledge (for example perhaps you have engaged in some part-time care work, or read about schizophrenia, depression or autism in order to better understand a friend's difficulties) then alluding to this appropriately in your form can only promote you as a serious applicant. Graduates are likely to be subject to greater scrutiny when it comes to justifying their decision to apply for psychology, and those who have gained paid or unpaid experience in care-related professions and who can demonstrate some relevant knowledge and understanding will be at an advantage.

Interviews

'The interview experience was a bit intimidating at first for me. I didn't know what to expect as it was not really like a job interview and I worried that I would be asked a lot of difficult questions about psychological theory. In fact the interviewers were more interested in my personal qualities and my capacity to reflect on my experiences. And it went very fast!'

Let us assume that you have completed and sent off your application – what next? The processes by which courses arrive at decisions of whether or not to interview candidates are at best impenetrable to those outside academia. Indeed, many universities' policies about interviewing appear to change by the year, with some offering places without interview, some interviewing most applicants and some interviewing only a select few before then making offers. Again, check with individual courses for details of their intentions about interviewing, including the likely dates: you don't want to find yourself in the position of having been offered an interview only to realise that it is to be held when you are away on a pre-paid package holiday to Ibiza or undergoing expensive root canal treatment.

BPP
LEARNING MEDIA

If some universities routinely do not interview but instead offer open days or other chances to talk to staff and students, it is in your interest to take up such offers. If you are going to spend several years (and possibly thousands of pounds) on a particular course, the least you want to know is whether or not you like the look of the university, the staff and the students, and the city. Having contact with courses – directly, via visits; or indirectly via agreed telephone discussions – can provide an ideal opportunity for finding out information that you might otherwise have asked about at interview.

Your information-gathering about courses should allow you to prepare yourself fully should you be called for interview. If you are called, then this is an invaluable opportunity to have some control over how you present yourself and to impress course representatives. Schools and colleges will provide prospective undergraduates with information and advice about how to approach interviews, as will friends and family. Graduate applicants will probably have more experience of interviews but may be no less anxious than undergraduates about the process because of what they have invested in this life change.

Personal qualities that interviewers will be looking for include academic ability, good communication skills, an interested and enquiring mind and an ability to think psychologically – ie to reflect on what is known about human experience and behaviour and to place your own experience and that of others within the context of such knowledge. Willingness to reconsider your perspectives in the light of counterarguments and contradictory evidence will also be positively received, as will a demonstrable capacity for caring and warmth – this is psychology, after all.

Having had months to prepare for the possible eventuality of being interviewed, you really should be ready to answer several likely questions:

- Why do you want to read psychology?

- Why do you want to read psychology at this university?

- What, do you think, makes you a suitable candidate?

- In what ways have your A level choices contributed to your decision to apply to study psychology?

In addition, you should have interesting things to say about your A level courses and be ready to field academic questions about specific areas of them. More demanding, perhaps, will be any general questions about you, your life experiences to date, your motivations and your ultimate goals. These may require more thought and preparation. When considering answers to likely interview questions you don't

want to develop highly elaborate, scripted material which, while it may make perfect sense to you, when delivered sounds over-rehearsed and doesn't in fact answer exactly what the interviewer is asking you. If you do over-rehearse specific answers you'll run the risk of relying totally on memory – and not thinking more broadly – and then getting into a panic, and all sorts of knots, if you forget certain points or the order in which you learned them. This really isn't a helpful approach to interviews at all. Far preferable is that you rehearse general themes and a range of specific points, keeping your material sufficiently flexible so you can select appropriately from it when deciding what you need in order to answer questions. Remember, there is nothing wrong at all with being transparent about having to think about your answers in an interview.

Make sure you have some questions to ask tutors, for when you are given the traditional opportunity to do so at the end of the interview. These questions should be relevant (ie, they should not simply reflect that you have failed to read the course prospectus) and make you sound interested. That said, it is not advisable to try to engage tutors in discussion on random, highly esoteric points apropos of nothing; that would, transparently, be a case of trying too hard.

Finally, it may be reassuring to remember that although you are at a nerve-wracking stage of your life, it is also an exciting one. Whether this is the only step you take in psychology and you then enter employment in another area, or whether you take further steps leading to a career as a psychology practitioner or researcher, what you're about to learn will always be interesting and have relevance because it's all about you and everyone you'll ever meet. How many subjects can offer that?

Chapter summary

Depending on your life experiences and previous academic qualifications, there are two routes to studying psychology: completing an undergraduate degree or a conversion diploma course. This chapter offers some tips and advice on how to complete the relevant application forms in order to make your case stand out and how to prepare for and succeed in the interview process.

Key points

- Talk to as many people as you can who are studying for, or who have completed, a psychology degree and any individuals you know who are practising psychologists, so that you can glean information untainted by spin – find out what people who are in the know *really* think about the field.

- Familiarise yourself with information about the application process and course accreditation provided by UCAS and the BPS.

- Read course prospectuses and compare and evaluate the merits of different courses and course modules, taking care to note whether or not courses are accredited.

- Note the academic and other entry requirements of particular courses to avoid wasting a vote applying for a course whose entry criteria you won't meet.

- Visit universities you are interested in as far as is possible, preferably on official open days.

- Try to gain some experience – voluntary or paid; even if it is only shadowing staff In care-related or other psychology-related work (this is especially important if you are a graduate hoping to convert).

- Put in some serious time and effort when completing your application form and get others to cast a constructively critical eye over it.

- Prepare thoroughly for interview.

Useful resources

Information on psychology careers:
www.bps.org.uk/careers-education-training
www.psychology.about.com/od/careersinpsychology

University and Colleges Admissions Service:
www.ucas.ac.uk

Chapter 4

Life as a psychology student

Dr Myrto Tsakopoulou

Following the relief of securing a place on a psychology course, you may be filled with anticipation about what life will be like as a student. You will probably receive most of the information you need in a pack with the university offer letter. This pack of information usually contains details about accommodation, enrolment dates, university facilities and the support services that will be available to you during your course. This chapter takes this a step further and provides an overview of some of the basic essentials you will need as a new psychology student, including preparations before the course and information that will help you manage during your time at university.

Preparation

Open days

It is a good idea to learn about and prepare for your university before you start the course. Open days are a great opportunity to familiarise yourself with the location of the university, get a feel for the place and meet some of the course tutors or psychology students who are currently doing the course. This will also allow you to check out the accommodation available to new students as well as the facilities that will be available to you. Attending the open day could help you ease your way into student life in the crucial first few days at university.

Accommodation

Year 1 students usually have priority for on-campus accommodation. It is highly recommended to take advantage of this opportunity, as it is a good way to meet other students of your year, make new friends and be near the university facilities. Check out all the accommodation information provided by your university in advance and ensure you sign up for it early, as there may be a lot of competition for places. Keep your options open with off-campus or private accommodation, which may be better quality than student halls, but it may limit your opportunities for meeting other first year students.

Get connected

You may have the opportunity to get in contact with other Year 1 students before you start. Most universities can give you access to online chat-rooms or contact details of other students once you get accepted by the course. Use this as an opportunity to get in contact early on. Even if you don't ever get to meet these people in real life, it could help to find out that other first years share similar feelings about starting university.

What to bring

There are a number of things that may come in handy at the start of your course but do not overload yourself. Think practically. Check if there is internet access in your accommodation and decide whether you will bring a computer or laptop with you. If you do, you can access books and journals online so you don't have to bring many books with you. Also it may be a good idea to wait until you are given a list of essential reading for the course, rather than buying books you may not end up using very much. Think about bringing practical items (eg multiplugs, desk-lamp, hangers) or some decorations and items that will make it feel like home. Most student halls are very basic and they will feel empty and cold when you first move in. Put your personal touch on your new home, but do not overdo it to begin with, as your tastes may change during your university years.

Freshers' week

This is the very first week you arrive at the university. It is an induction week organised with first year students (or 'freshers') in mind. During this week you will receive details about your course schedule, you will find out when lectures start and be given information about the facilities available to you. Primarily, however, you will be given the opportunity to meet new people and make friends. Activities during Freshers' week are organised by universities for that purpose: to help new students socialise and to establish a supportive network. The first days at university are usually very daunting for most people, and it is more than likely that most people you meet will be as nervous and shy as you are.

During this week you will start settling into your new room, meeting your flatmates and getting your bearings around the university and local area. There will usually be activities to help you with just that: club nights, day activities, and opportunities to sign up with different societies. It is a good idea to make the most of these opportunities: invite your flatmates into your room for a chat, join them in the kitchen, or plan to go out for a drink with them. Talk to as many people as possible when you are out and join societies that you may find interesting. If you are not British, the chances are there will be a society for people from your home country. Or you may have a specific interest in photography, tennis or paranormal activity. There are societies and clubs for everyone.

Top tips

Surviving Freshers' week:

- During this week you will probably be very tempted to stay in your room all day and night chatting to your friends from home online. Do not do it! Get out and talk to new people.

- Get to know your flatmates: leave your room door open, play some music or offer to make them some food or a cup of tea.

- Sign up with societies, activities and clubs you find interesting.

- Don't spend all your money on alcohol in the first week. Budget for the essentials and think about setting up a 'kitty' with your flatmates to share cost.

- Don't fall in love with the first person you meet! Keep your options open and be safe.

- It is normal to feel anxious and lonely in the first week. Most people do. Just because you want to be a psychologist and help other people with their problems it doesn't mean you shouldn't ask for help yourself. Talk to your friends, call a helpline or even cry to your mum on the phone. But remember: it will definitely get better and you will probably meet some of your future best friends during this time.

Case study

'Between and about the actual arranged activities of Freshers' week there's the stuff of real life to deal with: living independently – possibly for the first time; managing finances; calibrating and keeping to timetables and routines; negotiating emerging friendships; discovering new environments, etc. This is fertile territory, indeed, for making excruciating mistakes and presenting yourself as a monumental loon and general anti-magnet where desirable friendships are concerned. Just one embarrassing example from my own first week as an undergraduate that's worth offering: on my second day at university I returned to Woolworths the brilliantly large, curiously patterned cereal bowl I'd bought the day before and irritably explained that my milk and cornflakes had spewed all over my trousers through a hole in the base, only to have my clownish pomposity elicit the beautifully measured, crushing retort: "Yes sir: that's because you bought a plant pot…"' **Mark, who survived Freshers' week and is now a fully fledged clinical psychologist**

University facilities

Psychology learning facilities

During your course you will attend lectures, seminars and clinical labs. The lectures are usually attended by everyone from your year, while for the seminars and labs students are divided in smaller groups. Seminars and labs will give you the opportunity to discuss more critically and put theory into practice. The labs are usually a very interesting and engaging way to learn about important psychology experiments and theories.

Personal tutors

Most universities also provide personal tutors for each student, who follow your progress and to whom you can go to if you have any concerns or needs around your studies. Some courses offer you the opportunity to have the same tutor assigned to you throughout your studies. This can be an invaluable experience as a tutor may be able to offer you access to work placements, research projects, publications, work shadowing and they can provide you with references for jobs and further specialist training courses.

Library and e-learning

Most universities have libraries equipped with books, journals, magazines and any other periodicals that may be needed for your studies. They usually have a few copies of the most essential and popular books that you will be able to borrow for short or longer term periods. You should also be able to access the library catalogue online via your user login, where you can renew your loans. Most universities will give you access to e-journals and databases, where you will be able to download journal articles online. You should also be able to use inter-library facilities, where you can order books or any other learning resources which your library may not hold.

IT

You will have access to computing facilities on-site and most universities now offer free wi-fi internet access for students. Usually on enrolment you will be given a username and password along with instructions on how to join the university network. There will be allocated computer rooms for you to use or you can use your laptop in your own room.

Students' union

The students' union is a union representing students and it is usually a building or area within the university which houses entertainment centres, social learning areas and facilities. These are usually run by students for students. There you are likely to find a bar, advice centre and societies' areas. It may be a good idea to join the students' union as it will give you invaluable information and support in student matters. It will also give you access to student discounts!

Career advice

Most universities have a career advice centre, where they offer one-to-one advice on future career plans. Advisors will give you support and information on what skills you will need to develop to increase your chances for employment, how to develop your CV and how to prepare for interviews. They may be able to advise you on local volunteering services where you can develop and enhance your psychology skills or get you in contact with psychology graduates who can give you tips on your first steps towards employment.

'During my first year at university I approached the career advice centre and I was surprised by the level of help I received there. They helped me put my first CV together, gave me information on how to prepare for interviews and they gave me good guidance on where to look for psychology jobs. It was very helpful in building up my confidence in these early stages of my professional development.'

Catering and shops

It is very likely that your university will have shops, restaurants and bars that provide for students and staff, especially if it is on campus. These facilities sometimes provide food, drinks and groceries at lower or competitive prices to cater for students.

Chaplaincy and spirituality

University chaplaincies are usually multi-faith and they offer a space for reflection, prayer and worship to students. There you can usually access support, advice and activities provided by staff from a variety of religious backgrounds.

Counselling

Most universities offer counselling support to students who may experience emotional difficulties and need to speak to someone. There are usually counselling services that can offer short- or long-term psychological support; they can refer you to more suitable psychological services if needed or they can offer you advocacy and advice if your difficulties are affecting your studies. As a student you will also have access to Nightline, which is an out-of-hours telephone support service run by students for students. This is also a service where you can volunteer as a psychology student and gain some valuable experience which can enhance your CV.

Sports

There will be many opportunities to get involved in sports activities during your studies. If your university has a campus, there will usually be a sports centre and facilities for a variety of sports. Or you may be entitled to access local sports centres at a discounted price. There will be a number of sports-related societies and clubs where you can get in touch with other students with similar interests and join a team. This is an excellent way to keep fit, healthy and to socialise.

Societies

Societies and activity clubs are an integral part of university life. These are social groups usually set up and run by students for students. They are set up with a common interest shared by its members, from philosophy, to wall-climbing, films and bird-watching. When you join you will meet people with the same interest and meet them on planned social gatherings or outings. It is a great opportunity to meet people, socialise and expand your learning. There are societies to cover most interests. But if you cannot find what you are looking for, you can always set up your own!

Top tips when joining societies

- Beware the undiscriminating welcome sometimes offered by the recruiting personnel of some religious groups – many of whom will relentlessly pursue those who show an interest. Any group – religious or otherwise – that refuses to accept, instantly, your ambivalence or change of heart is a group to be wary of.

- Collect others' details but be cautious about handing over yours! Get the information you want, and agree to get back to others if, after reflection, you're interested. Do not hand over any bank details – ever – to anyone, before thoroughly checking they're legitimate.

- Remain mindful that confidence tricksters from outside of the university will be circling like sharks, ready to perform scams on inexperienced and unsuspecting students.

- Budget! Look at your income, and consider the outgoings you're about to incur if you're bent on becoming an active member of everything from the 'Air balloon-bursting Club' to the 'Zappa Appreciation Society'.

Chapter summary

Student life can be challenging and demanding, not only academically but also emotionally and financially. Most students will be filled with anxiety when they first arrive at university but there will be a lot of activities, facilities and support to help you cope with the demands. You will have many opportunities to meet new people, socialise and learn along the way. You are very likely to make some of your closest future friends during your studies and to have many good life experiences.

Key points

- Good preparation will make your transition to student life easier. Read the information provided by your university before you start and take all relevant actions early, from applying for accommodation to signing up for your university pass.

- Make the most of Freshers' week. This is set up to help you meet new people and to find out more about the university facilities that will be available to you.

- Most universities are equipped with facilities to cover most of your needs or they will provide you with information with how to access them outside the university. The students' union is usually a good place to find out more about what is available to you.

Useful resources

More information on Freshers' week and university life:
www.nus.org.uk/en/students-unions
www.gov.uk/browse/education
UniversityAndHigherEducation/LifeAtUniversityOrCollege/index.htm
www.mind.org.uk/help/diagnoses_and_conditions/stress_of_student_life
www.studentastic.co.uk
www.thestudentroom.co.uk/wiki/Fresher's_Week_Tips

Chapter 5

Planning your finances

Maria Tzortzaki

Making the decision to study psychology involves several steps which have been discussed in previous chapters. However one of the main issues you will come across when entering higher education is the expense involved. A degree is a great investment in your future, and managing your money properly when you get to university will be crucial to surviving financially. This chapter will give you an overview of the main costs involved in studying for an undergraduate degree in the UK, and will provide you with information on funding opportunities. Budgeting ideas discussed can help you keep a good balance between worrying too much about money and fully enjoying the university experience.

Tuition fees

Tuition fees are an important consideration when you choose an undergraduate degree. The amount charged by UK universities to home students will see a significant increase in 2012–2013 as a response to changes in the way the government funds higher education. In 2010–2011 the average fees paid for undergraduate psychology courses were £3,323 a year, whereas students were expected to pay variable annual tuition fees (up to £3,375) for psychology courses in 2011–12. However for 2012–2013 universities have introduced fee tariffs up to £9,000 a year with an average of £8,500 for an undergraduate degree in psychology (*The Guardian*, 2011). Universities in Scotland, Wales and Northern Ireland are also able to raise their fees from 2012, but their home students will not be affected. It is worth mentioning that Scottish universities often offer four-year courses that lead to an undergraduate master of arts (MA) degree. If you are an international student, the fees you pay are not directly affected by government funds in higher education as they already cover the full cost of teaching. For overseas students fees vary from £7,000 up to £16,000 per year depending on the institution.

Living costs

In addition to tuition fees you should consider the living costs involved in going to university. Your overall expenditure budget should also allow for costs that include amongst others:

*   Accommodation
*   Food
*   Transport
*   Entertainment
*   Other miscellaneous
*   Visas, vacation costs and airfares (for international and EU students)

Whether you travel to and from university at the start and end of term, or stay there for the duration of the vacations, these additional travel or accommodation costs will need to be covered. UKCISA (The UK Council for International Student Affairs) has teamed up with UNIAID, an independent charity helping students cope with finance. They have come up with an online tool to help students budget and manage their finances better. The international student calculator online tool enables you to build a personalised budget, get information on areas like insurance, banking and cost of living, and learn from case studies and top tips from students.

Top tip

- Try out MoneySavingExpert.com, a forum for students to discuss money advice and tips: www.moneysavingexpert.com/students/student-finance-calculator

---

Accommodation

Several types of accommodation are available to you as a student. However cost, comfort, and location are likely to determine which one you opt for.

Halls of residence

Halls of residence are large student dormitories with self-contained rooms. Some have their own bathroom and kitchen, others have shared facilities. Rent is split into termly amounts and is paid at the beginning of each term. Heating, gas, electricity, water, insurance, basic cleaning and a high speed internet connection are on most occasions included in the rent. Most universities offer both catered and self-catered accommodation. What this means is that you can either have your meals included in the accommodation (catered) or be responsible for your own cooking (self-catered). In terms of cost, on average you should allow £105 per week for nine months (term time). These costs are for a single-study bedroom. Actual costs will depend on your type of accommodation, and most universities will often have dedicated sections on their websites that give an estimate of the cost of on-campus accommodation. Halls of residence are usually the number one choice of first year students, as they are reasonably priced, and give you time to settle in the university environment and make friends.

'As a first year student, living in halls was a fantastic experience. It was a great chance to meet people outside my course and to make friends. It also allowed me to settle in to university life quickly, and to become more independent. You get a real sense of community in halls and that is quite important when you move away from home for the first time.'

Privately rented accommodation

Privately rented accommodation costs vary depending on the number of people you share with and the quality and location of the accommodation. On average you should allow £120 per week. As might be expected, accommodation cost is likely to be higher for London and some other cities in the UK. The 'Accommodation for Students' website provides full figures for the cost of private halls and off-campus shared houses in student areas across the country (see Useful resources). Another option is renting a private flat, however these are generally expensive and out of reach for most students.

Food, entertainment and travel

Your food costs will vary depending on taste and dietary needs, but will account for a significant part of the budget. Most campuses offer a choice of places – restaurants, bars, cafes, that provide everything from a sandwich to a main meal well at reasonable prices. What is important to consider, is that even in catered halls you will need to buy lunches. As for entertainment, different options will be available depending on the location of the university. Very often entertainment in the students' union is subsidised, and so are events organised by university societies and clubs. A rough estimate of weekly expenses would be £80 for housekeeping (food, toiletries etc) and entertainment.

In terms of travel, many halls of residence are located either on, or very close to the university campuses. The ability to walk to lecture halls and other facilities greatly reduces travel costs. When this is not possible, universities often arrange special travel rates with local bus companies for students during term time. In larger cities you can benefit from student discounts on reduced rail fares, for example in London the TfL/ National Rail Student Oyster photocard scheme will save you 30% off all adult travelcards and bus passes valid for a week.

Top tips

Things to try out:

- Do your own cooking – using the kitchens in halls of residences is great for socialising with friends.
- Take advantage of student discounts – look out for student discounts in cinema, theatre and other entertainment venues.
- Reduce day-to-day travel costs – walk where possible and sign up for reduced rail and bus fares.

Course costs

As an undergraduate student your general study costs will include but will not be limited to books, stationery and photocopying. Some undergraduate degrees in psychology may involve lab work, so it is possible that you will have to budget for that additional cost. Also, thinking ahead for the final year of your studies, dissertation requirements may increase normal spending on printing and photocopying. In addition to this, some additional travel costs may arise in the event that you decide to conduct a field research study or experiment. However good budgeting can help you keep these costs to the minimum. Some ideas involve buying second-hand text books online or from students in the year above and using IT facilities and offers provided by your university. As with food and entertainment, don't forget to make the most of student discounts.

Top tip

- The NUS (National Union of Students) Extra card costs £11 and entitles you to exclusive discounts for almost everything, from food and drink to books and computer equipment: www.nus.org.uk.

Student memberships

The British Psychological Society (BPS) is the main body that represents psychologists in the UK however as a psychology student you don't necessarily need to be a member while studying. If you choose a psychology degree that is BPS accredited you will be able to apply for student membership. Some benefits of joining the BPS as a student member include exclusive discounts to books, journals and events, the chance to transfer to graduate membership free of charge after completing your undergraduate degree, as well as access to *The Psychologist* magazine and *PsychTalk* newsletter written by students.

BPP
LEARNING MEDIA

Top tip

- Apply for the annual subscription for student members of the BPS. You will need to pay £54, as an annual fee, but discounts may apply to those not earning a taxable income.

Case study

John knew that moving to London to study would mean that he would have to get by on a very tight budget. Besides applying for a bursary and a student maintenance grant he made full use of student deals. John equipped himself with a young person's railcard and other student discounts for travel. During Fresher's week, he signed up for student deals and started using discount websites to buy tickets for gigs online. He also shared supermarket shopping with his housemates, to save money on food. Living in London on a student budget was nowhere near as bad as John had anticipated.

Estimating your income

Student loans

A number of financial support options are available to new undergraduate students. The UK government, via the Student Loans Company (SLC), can provide loans to help with your tuition fees as long as you meet the eligibility criteria outlined on the GOV.UK website (see Useful resources). What this means is that you will be supported in borrowing up to the full cost of your tuition fees which will be paid directly by the government to your university of choice. You will need to apply for this loan before you arrive at university and you can do this through the GOV.UK student finance page. Although paying the new increased fees can be daunting, you need to remember that you will only start repaying this loan once you have left your course and are earning over £21,000. Another point to keep in mind is that from the date you take out a student loan you will be charged interest at the rate of inflation plus 3%. Once you have graduated or otherwise left the university you will be charged interest at the rate of inflation (if you are earning less than £21,000), or the rate of inflation plus up to 3% (if you are earning between £21,001 and £41,000) or the rate of inflation plus 3% (if you are earning above £41,000). Check 'the student calculator' online tool to get a better idea of how you can repay your loan. Also you can get further information about interest rates and repayment details of student loans on the GOV.UK website.

BPP
LEARNING MEDIA

As you already know, paying for fees is only one of the costs involved in studying. For this reason, money is also available for eligible full-time students to pay for things such as rent, food and bills. The government provides student maintenance loans, and all full-time home students can apply for up to 65% of the maximum amount to cover living costs. You can get a proportion of the loan regardless of your household income, whereas another proportion is available depending on family income. The maintenance loan aims to cover living costs during the academic year and will be paid into your student account in three instalments – one at the start of each term. The maximum amounts are £5,500 for students living away from home outside of London, £7,675 for students living away from home in London, and £4,375 for students living at home.

Top tip

- Useful information for students and parents regarding student finance for undergraduates: www.gov.uk/browse/education/student-finance

Grants and bursaries

As a full-time student you can also apply for a combination of maintenance grants, bursaries and scholarships offered by the government, universities and colleges, or other organisations like charities and businesses.

If you are a student from a lower-income household starting your course in 2012–2013 you may be able to get a maintenance grant or special support grant of up to £3,250 a year, which you don't have to repay. The way this is decided is by means testing, which is where they look at how much your household earns each year, usually based on your parents' income. The full amount is available for students with a household income of £25,000 per year or less. If your household income is between £25,000 and £42,600 you will be able to get some grant, although the higher your household income the less you get. The maintenance grant and the special support grant are paid to you by student finance direct at the start of each term. You will get the grant at the same time as any student loan for maintenance. In order for you to get a maintenance grant you will need to have your household income assessed. If you visit the GOV.UK website you can read more about how and also when to apply for student finance support.

In addition to the financial support you can receive from the government, most universities have significantly increased the number of bursaries and scholarships offered to students starting their courses in 2012–2013.

Similarly to maintenance grants, support from bursaries and scholarships does not have to be repaid. They are awarded to different students for different reasons such as your household income, how well you have done in your exams and the type of school (ie state, independent) you attended. Some universities might offer a reduction on your fees or a fee waiver instead. Whatever your circumstances it is advisable that you investigate the different scholarships / bursaries provided by universities you are interested in applying to. You will find that the funding opportunities provided may vary, in number of scholarships / bursaries available, an element that may influence your decision.

If you are an international student, you will not be eligible for any financial assistance from the UK government. As a first step you will need to contact your home country to determine if there is any financial support available. Some UK universities offer country specific scholarships, and work in partnership with other countries to enable international students to access financial support from their home country.

Funding opportunities include:

* Student loans
* Maintenance grant and special support grant
* Bursaries, scholarships and awards
* Financial support for international students

Other sources of funding

Part-time work

Many students supplement their income when studying by getting a part-time job or working in the summer holidays. Balancing full-time study and part-time work is demanding, and will have an impact on the lifestyle you can afford as a student. Nonetheless it provides valuable skills that are helpful for getting a job later on. During term time you will need to be realistic about the hours you can work. Most universities would recommend that you work no more than 15 hours per week, so it does not affect your study.

Scholarships / bursaries for postgraduate students

For students interested in postgraduate study in psychology, or those who may have particular research interests, key sources of non-repayable funding are available from research councils, government departments, loans, trusts and charities, and business and industry. Universities always aim to attract talent and will offer scholarships and

bursaries to students to give them the opportunity to study regardless of their financial circumstances. Most of these scholarships are achievement-based, so do check your eligibility by visiting the funding website of your university of choice. The British Psychological Society (BPS) also offers some awards for postgraduate psychologists, and although it doesn't provide student bursaries, the 'funding opportunities database' available on the BPS website will give you details of various funding options.

Bank loans for postgraduate students

If you decide to take on a loan to complete your postgraduate study in psychology, you could look into the Professional and Career Development Loan. This is a deferred repayment bank loan set at a competitive fixed interest rate that can be used to support learning or training that enhances your job or career prospects. A Professional and Career Development Loan is essentially a bank loan, but the Learning and Skills Council (LSC) will pay the interest on the loan during the agreed course dates and one month afterwards. This means that the loan is interest-free during your studies. The loan can help to fund a wide range of courses, including psychology, lasting up to two years. You may borrow between £300 and £10,000 from a participating bank, which can be put towards covering tuition fees, course-related costs or living expenses. The difference between this and undergraduate student loan, is that the Professional and Career Development Loan must be repaid at the end of the training, regardless of your employment status.

Chapter summary

Getting a university degree is a fantastic investment in your future but it doesn't come for free. This chapter has given you an overview of the various costs involved. It has looked at living and course expenses as well as student loans and funding options provided by the government and other institutions. Further resources are included below to help you get more information and fully explore the support you can receive and opportunities available so that you can make the most of the university experience on a budget!

Key points

- When planning your finances make sure you consider all costs involved.
- Budgeting is key, use the suggested online tools to calculate your average expenses.
- Get to grips with student loans, the more you know about them the less daunting they sound.

Useful resources

The Site.org offers information and advice on funding available to students: www.thesite.org/homelawandmoney/money/studentmoney

International Student Calculator is a tool designed to help international students studying in the UK manage their funds: www.international.studentcalculator.org.uk/international

Accommodation for Students is a search engine that enables you to look for accommodation around the UK: www.accommodationforstudents.com

GOV.UK is the official government website when applying for government funding: www.gov.uk/browse/education/student-finance

Universities and Colleges Admissions Service (Great Britain and Northern Ireland): www.ucas.ac.uk

Central Applications Office (Republic of Ireland):
www.cao.ie

NUS Extra (savings and discounts for students):
www.nus.org.uk/en/nus-extra

The Student Room (topics specifically on money and finance issues):
www.thestudentroom.co.uk

Funding options

Prospects (the UK's official website for graduates careers provides information on funding options for postgraduate study):
www.prospects.ac.uk

GOV.UK (funding opportunities for postgraduate study):
www.gov.uk/funding-for-postgraduate-study

Postgraduate studentships:
www.postgraduatestudentships.co.uk

Reference

Sedghi, A and Shepherd, J (2011) *Tuition fees 2012: what are the universities charging?* [Online] Available at:
www.guardian.co.uk/education [Accessed 5 March 2012].

Chapter 6

What does studying psychology involve?

Dr Sokratis Dinos

Studying psychology can be a very rewarding experience provided that you:

*   Plan and schedule your study time
*   Study actively
*   Are active in class
*   Are a good team player and can work effectively in groups

The majority of undergraduate psychology courses provide you with a sound foundation in all the key areas of psychology and specialist fields including cognitive, biological, developmental, social, clinical, health, organisational, forensic and neuroscience.

Undergraduate courses are designed with equal focus on theory, empirical research and ethics and with the view to cover the field of psychology as widely as possible in order to provide you with the necessary professional skills that you will need to become a psychologist. The overarching aim of a good psychology course is to provide you with knowledge and understanding of the core areas of psychology extending to more advanced specialist fields and their application.

Any BSc Psychology course is largely grounded in systematic empirical research as well as in theory; it therefore includes training in methods of research, which in turn demands some understanding of, and some skill in, statistics and computing.

Top tip

Research methods and data analysis skills will give you the opportunity to apply yourself in many different vocational contexts within and outside of psychology including academic / research, social policy, health and epidemiology and market research to name a few.

The course will also enable you to present theoretical arguments, research results and general ideas in a cogent and critical manner. These are intellectual and practical skills which are potentially relevant to a wide range of occupations in our society and the job market.

Structure of a psychology course

An undergraduate degree in psychology covers three years of taught material. However, many universities provide what is called a sandwich degree. The sandwich degree is a four-year undergraduate course in which you will undertake a placement year in industry, normally after the second year at university (see Chapter 2). Normally, the first two years of your degree broadly cover the field of psychology. The third (or

fourth year if you are in a sandwich course) year is very often designed to offer considerable choice of topics for study.

As highlighted in other chapters, you should be aware of the British Psychological Society (BPS) and the fact that the majority of BSc Psychology courses are accredited by the BPS. Accreditation of degrees is done by following a number of BPS requirements, which cover aspects from course content to facilities. A number of modules throughout your undergraduate degree will have been accredited by the BPS and are most often referred to as core modules within your degree specification. All psychology undergraduate degrees cover these modules at some point. Also note that these core modules may appear under different module names depending on the course and university but the content is very similar. A description of each of these modules is provided later on in this chapter.

Year 1 of your psychology degree

Although there can be variations, most courses provide an introduction to biological psychology, cognitive psychology, developmental psychology, social psychology, and research methods and statistics in psychology. Very often during the first year of your studies you will also be taught conceptual and historical issues in psychology. All these areas are often referred to as core areas. Normally by the end of the first year of your studies, you will develop:

- A knowledge and understanding of some of the core areas in psychology
- A knowledge of the research paradigms and methods used in the practical application of psychology and evaluate the research literature appropriately
- A knowledge of and demonstrate ability in using basic statistical techniques and in reporting research findings using statistical analysis software
- An ability to write essays and reports in a cohesive manner while demonstrating knowledge of the subject matter appropriately
- An ability to argue logically based on empirical evidence
- The transferable skills of communication, team work and autonomous learning

Year 2 of your psychology degree

During the second year of your studies you will progress to a more challenging and in-depth reflection on some of the topics you covered in the first year, as well as being introduced to some new subjects. This

is also the time when you will start to reflect on the topics that you are interested in with the aim of identifying one to form your dissertation in the final year of your studies. By the end of Year 2 of your studies, you will develop:

- The foundations of the cognitive and practical skills necessary for becoming a psychologist, including analysis, evaluation, synthesis, problem-solving and research skills
- An understanding of scientific insights into human behaviour
- An ability to analyse and evaluate arguments succinctly
- The transferable skills of communication, team work and autonomous learning

It is also during the second and third year that BPS accredits a number of modules, which form the basis for Graduate Basis for Chartership (see Chapter 2 for BPS accreditation). In particular, any BPS accredited course will have to meet the following requirements:

- The core domains associated with the GBC curriculum and therefore included in any BPS accredited course are: biological psychology, cognitive psychology, developmental psychology, social psychology, conceptual and historical issues in psychology, research methods, individual differences and final year empirical project.
- The course is very much grounded in research methods, evidence-based teaching and ethical procedures, which also form part of the BPS guidelines.

Top tip

All BPS accredited courses (including conversion courses) must provide coverage of seven core areas in psychology (and a final year empirical project). These are:

- Biological psychology
- Conceptual and historical issues in psychology
- Cognitive psychology
- Developmental psychology
- Personality and individual differences
- Research methods
- Social psychology
- Final year empirical project (dissertation)

During the first two years of your studies you will normally be introduced to a wide range of topics that may inspire you and help shape your ideas for research, which you will need for your dissertation in the final year.

Top tip

The earlier you start to formulate your ideas for your final project the better. It is also advisable to discuss your ideas with members of faculty who will help to ensure that:

- The research question, hypothesis, objectives and / or aims of your topic (including sampling) are appropriate; and

- Any ethical issues and / or requirements have been considered and steps taken to make sure you meet any such requirements (including both internal and external approval).

Year 3 (final year) of your psychology degree

The aim of a good psychology course is to provide you with an integrated academic and professional training environment conceived and structured to enable you to gain the knowledge, understanding and skills to pursue and sustain a career in psychology. By the end of Year 3, you would be expected to:

- Develop knowledge and understanding of the discipline of psychology including the ability to reflect on the historical, conceptual, cultural, social and political evolution of the discipline

- Have a critical understanding of the discipline of psychology with an emphasis on the empirical study of mind, brain, and behaviour, including hypothesis-testing, information-handling, synthesis, problem-solving and the critical evaluation of empirical data

- Reflect on, assess and apply robust ethical procedures to your work and research conduct including data collection and analysis

- Apply psychological theory to everyday life situations, experience and behaviour

- Develop a range of more general practical and transferable skills in problem-solving, effective communication, personal development and autonomous learning, so as to facilitate access to a broad range of educational and employment opportunities after graduation

Empirical project (dissertation) and supervision in your final year

During the final year of your studies you will also undertake a substantial piece of independent research as part of your dissertation. The topic of your psychology project needs to fall within the field of psychology and is normally discussed and agreed with your academic supervisor. Your supervisor's role is to manage all the stages of the process to complete your dissertation and to guide you but all the thinking and input needs to be yours. In particular, you are expected to produce your literature searches, literature review and discussion without much input from your supervisor. The areas that your supervisor provides more guidance on are in:

- Shaping of literature review and research questions in order to make sure that these are viable to answer

- Conducting your data collection in an ethical manner

- Managing your data including practical advice on data analysis

- Reporting of the results following academic protocols of methodology and reporting

Top tip

Depending on the quality of your work, and after you have submitted your dissertation, your supervisor may encourage you to present your work at student and other conferences. You may also be encouraged to publish your work with your supervisor who will very often be leading the process of writing up and submitting for publication.

Ethical clearance for your dissertation

Once the topic of your empirical project has been agreed with your supervisor, you will need to receive ethical clearance. Your supervisor will discuss the ethical implications with you and assist you with your application. Normally, ethics applications are submitted to the university's ethics committee. Ethics committees tend to meet regularly and review applications from students who wish to conduct research with human participants.

In some cases, you will need to apply for ethical clearance to a local research ethics committee (LREC). This will be the case if your project involves recruitment of NHS participants and you should discuss this with your supervisor once your research project has been approved.

Psychology undergraduate curriculum

The core modules that are part of the majority of psychology courses and which are also compulsory BPS modules are as follows. (You can also find these listed in the second Top tip of the Chapter.)

Biological psychology

This module introduces the basics of cell anatomy and neural transmission and explains how information is communicated through the role of various neurotransmitters in the body. In addition the module may explore how disorders such as schizophrenia and drug addiction can be studied and explained at the level of neural activity. The module may further cover topic areas including sleep, emotion, language, memory, disorders such as Parkinson's disease and may provide an historical perspective on the advances in brain science. Biological research methods such as brain imaging techniques (for example PET, fMRI, EEG), physiological recording, and the study of brain-damaged patients are also part of this module.

Cognitive psychology

Cognitive psychology is concerned with the experimental analysis of mental processes and structures. In part, it is an attempt to provide an empirical science to replace 'folk psychology' regarding such mental concepts as attention, memory, perception, thought and language. It draws on a variety of ideas from information theory, philosophy of mind, neuroscience, logic, linguistics, and computer science.

Conceptual and historical issues in psychology

This module is designed to provide an in-depth understanding of the foundations of psychological thought by exploring historical and conceptual issues in psychology. Understanding how concepts and debates evolved and how they came to be incorporated into current psychological thought is essential. Furthermore, the module provides an introduction to all the schools of thought in psychology that have shaped psychology as a science.

Developmental psychology

This module explores the processes that shape our lives between conception and death. Although each life unfolds in its own unique pattern, the module explores the ways biological, psychological, and

BPP
LEARNING MEDIA

sociological influences systematically combine to shape its course. The module describes physical, cognitive, and social growth of people with special attention to various cultural contexts of development and the rich diversity of individuals. The content is drawn from research and theories in developmental psychology.

Personality and individual differences

The module introduces a range of theoretical approaches to personality and provides you with a review of personality, intelligence and individual differences. Topics that are normally covered in the module are paradigms of personality, the biological basis of our behaviour, the influence of environment and culture on our personality, how intelligence can be defined and measured, psychometric testing and personality and wellbeing.

Research methods and statistics in psychology

Research plays an essential role in business and in public policy and practice. Both commercial firms and government institutions rely upon research to inform their decisions, to test the effectiveness of existing policies, to predict the effects of intended future policies, to understand management processes and decisions, and to gain insights into public preferences and opinions about public services. The range of research issues and research methods available for researchers to use is complex and varied. Therefore, this module concentrates on helping you develop a thorough understanding of the key principles and practice of research that are needed to design and conduct a valid research project.

Along with research methods you will also be taught a great deal of statistics. Statistics and data analysis play a vital role in many fields of human activity – business, law, and psychology are among the fields that benefit from their use. Statistics are based on data and data is what we see, hear, perceive and so on. Such data is collected, organised, analysed, and interpreted so conclusions can be drawn. In other words, statistics are employed to transform data into useful information that can then be used for decisions to be made. Beyond a thorough understanding of the key terms of statistics, you will be taught and engage in statistical data analysis using statistical software. The majority of universities use SPSS software. However, there is other statistical software, which are preferred to SPPS such as Stata.

Social psychology

This module focuses on processes through which we construct an understanding of the world, develop a sense of self, and operate within groups. An important topic in social psychology is social cognition, which is concerned with how we acquire and process information, how we explain our own and others' behaviour and how these impact on our emotions, self-concept and relationship to others. Social psychology is also concerned with the notion of the self – where it comes from, what it is and how it affects thought and behaviour. Furthermore, during this module you will be looking at issues of group identification as well as intra- and inter-group behaviour and conflict and you will be discussing concepts such as social influence, conformity, obedience as well as the roles of the majority and minority.

Final year psychology project (also known as dissertation)

The final psychology project requires you to carry out your own research on a topic in psychology. This module normally carries the most weight in credit points and allows you to apply the knowledge acquired over the first two years and further develop your research, analytical and writing skills to investigate in-depth a topic of your choice. Therefore, this module aims to develop and train your understanding of the techniques of designing, conducting, analysing and interpreting your own empirical investigations using a critical appreciation of the principles of a good design as well as the conceptual and practical skills involved in data collection and analysis.

> 'During the first two years of my degree I had countless ideas about topics that I wanted to focus on. These ideas kept changing from one term to the next as I was being introduced to and was becoming knowledgeable in more areas. However, my ideas had been formed before the end of my second year, which gave me plenty of time to discuss my topic with various staff members and shape it even more. By the beginning of my third year I had a very clearly defined topic, a supervisor that I really liked and a proposal for a project. This gave me a whole year to conduct my dissertation and also gave me a great amount of pleasure researching a topic that I really liked without being under a lot of time pressure. My dissertation received a first and the whole experience has been very valuable to me.'

Specialist areas and modules in psychology

By and large, Years 1 and 2 of your studies cover the core modules, whereas Year 3 is more flexible and covers a number of other specialist areas. In most psychology degrees, the final year also gives you the opportunity to direct your studies towards those areas of psychology that you are most interested in, by giving you the option to:

- Develop specialist knowledge in specific areas of psychology according to your specific interest

- Gain a good understanding of some of the most contemporary specialist fields in psychology by choosing options from any of these specialist areas in order to find an area for future study or application that you are most interested in

Option modules may be subject to change over the duration of a degree course and others may be added. The specialist areas depend on the research interests / outputs of the department, the staff interests and also the focus that a department may have.

Top tip

If you already have some interest in a particular future career path and / or topic of research, check if the department shares the same interests with you. It is likely that a department will not allow you to pursue a line of research (for the empirical project in particular) if they feel that they lack the relevant academic knowledge or expertise.

Some of the most common specialist routes include:

Clinical and health psychology: there are a number of modules that can be taught in the context of this route. Some of the most popular modules that are taught in many university courses are:

- Health psychology (or psychology of health and illness): this module provides you with an overview of issues influencing health behaviours and also focuses on theories and models of behavioural change and illness cognition. Additionally, the concepts of health promotion and health behaviours (of eating, exercise, smoking cessation, alcohol addiction and stress management) may also be explored.

- Abnormal psychology (or psychology of mental illness or psychopathology): the field of psychopathology is one of the cornerstones of psychology and this module introduces you to the main diagnostic categories of mental illness in adults and children. The aim is to give you an overview of the major diagnostic classifications as well as symptoms and causes relating to mental illness taking into consideration biological, psychological and sociological explanations.

Cognitive psychology and cognitive neuroscience: which attempts to investigate and explain the neural mechanisms involved in cognitive processes. This area in psychology is rapidly expanding and some university departments specialise in this area with some excellent laboratory facilities for experiments. Although this specialist area is more common in postgraduate studies, some courses may include in their undergraduate curriculum:

- Introduction to cognitive neuroscience: this module introduces you to the methods used in research (eg EEG, PET, fMRI, TMS, eye-tracking, and brain lesion studies) and provides you with knowledge of functional and anatomical parts of the brain. The module may also include current research topics in cognitive neuroscience (eg perception and attention, action, emotion, memory, and executive functions) and may explore how research is applied to health (eg rehabilitation of patients who have suffered brain damage).

Organisational psychology: like cognitive neuroscience, this is an expanding specialist field in psychology. There are a number of different modules that can be taught in the context of this field but any courses with this field in their curriculum courses, would normally deliver:

- Introduction to organisational or occupational psychology: this module normally focuses on issues influencing the relationship of people and organisations at work. This field of psychological studies examines the frameworks and application of theories in organisations. Additionally, this module may explore issues of organisational change, job satisfaction and performance and personnel management.

Educational psychology: this is another popular field in psychology and like in the other specialist fields some departments are renowned for their specialisation and research output in this field. Educational psychology is an extension of the field of developmental psychology as applied to education. Education providers may include in their curriculum a module such as:

- Introduction to educational psychology (and / or special educational needs): this module normally explores the application of psychology to education and in particular the application of psychological theories on the cognitive, emotional and behavioural development of children and young people in a learning context, and more particularly in a school classroom. Theories and research findings concerning both the experience of the student and the teacher may also be examined with an emphasis on learning, assessing the student's learning / performance, creating an effective and enjoyable learning environment and working with developmentally gifted and disadvantaged students.

Forensic psychology: this is another popular specialist field in psychology. Some psychology departments have a strong background in the field in terms of research activity and outputs as well as delivering postgraduate degrees in the field. Such departments may offer modules that can be studied as an elective during your undergraduate degree. Such modules normally include:

- Introduction to forensic psychology: this module tends to focus on the clinical and individual oriented application of psychology within legal and criminal justice practices. The emphasis most often is on understanding both the offender and the role that the psychologist takes in the criminal justice system, from arrest and trial through to sentencing and release.

- Introduction to investigative psychology: this module places a greater emphasis on scientific methods and examination of process rather than the criminal actor *per se*. The focus is most often on the understanding of the psychological mechanisms that underpin the offender's behaviour and the similar principles which govern those charged with detecting and apprehending the offender, from crime incidence through to arrest and committal to trial.

The aforementioned specialist routes and the suggested modules are not definitive. Courses may choose to use different terminology to name a module and also there are other specialist fields in psychology such as positive psychology and political psychology. Therefore, make sure you do your research before you make up your mind which university and psychology course to apply for.

Case study

'Since I was at school I wanted to study psychology. From a very young age I was drawn to the subjects of ethnicity, culture, minorities and mental health, in particular. These topics fall under the remit of two different fields in psychology; social psychology and abnormal psychology. When I started studying psychology I turned all my focus to these modules (social, cultural, abnormal, clinical, health psychology) and on the other hand, I kind of made up my mind that I would not enjoy any of the other modules. We had a lot of statistics modules which I found quite difficult and I could not see any direct links with psychology. I also found biological psychology difficult and I did not want to see what the point in studying this was.

It was only when I decided to allow myself to have more of an open mind that I was pleasantly surprised. In particular, I fell in love with biological psychology; a subject which to my mind could not have been further removed from what interested me, but, in actuality was extremely relevant to the topic of mental health and ethnicity. I actually ended up doing my dissertation on biological psychology using some sophisticated statistical tools to analyse my data.

Much later I realised that one of the reasons I had made up my mind about what I would be focusing on during my degree was a fear that I would not understand subjects such as biology and statistics and an additional ignorance about what these subjects consisted of. I feel very lucky that I eventually gave my psychology subjects an equal chance as I believe that balanced or complete psychological knowledge requires input from different fields in psychology.'
John Edwards, Psychology Researcher

Chapter summary

A good psychology course is designed with equal focus on theory and empirical research and will provide you with knowledge of the core areas of psychology as well as more advanced specialist fields and their application. A BSc degree in Psychology spans over three years of taught material. In the first two years most psychology undergraduate degrees cover seven core modules in psychology such as biological, conceptual and historical, cognitive, developmental and social psychology as well as personality and individual differences, and research methods. In the final year, psychology degrees tend to be quite flexible in terms of providing a number of specialist routes (in addition to your final year empirical project which is compulsory if you are studying for a BSc or for GBC through BPS). Some of the most popular specialist routes include clinical, health, educational, organisational and / or forensic psychology. If you have some idea about or interest in some particular field or topic, it would be advisable to check if the department has expertise in this field / topic. A department that specialises in your field of interest may be more suitable for you than a department that is higher in the rankings.

Key points

- Years 1 and 2 of your studies tend to cover the core areas / modules in psychology, whereas the third year is more flexible and covers a number of other specialist areas.

- All BPS accredited courses (including conversion courses) must provide coverage of seven core areas in psychology. With the addition of a dissertation, these are:

    - Biological psychology
    - Conceptual and historical issues in psychology
    - Cognitive psychology
    - Developmental psychology
    - Personality and individual differences
    - Research methods
    - Social psychology

- Popular specialist fields in psychology that may be covered at an introductory level include clinical, health, organisational and forensic psychology.

- If you already have some interest in a particular future career path and / or topic of research, it is advisable that you aim for a department shares the same interests with you.

Useful resources

The British Psychological Society has general information about accredited psychology courses with links to the departmental websites, where you can look at the modules on offer: www.bps.org.uk

The Complete University Guide can give you an overview about universities in the UK which offer psychology degrees: www.thecompleteuniversityguide.co.uk

Chapter 7

What career paths are available with a psychology degree?

Maria Tzortzaki

When initially thinking about studying psychology many students assume that becoming a professional psychologist is the only career option available. However, what you should know is that many career paths are open to psychology graduates and they are definitely worth exploring. This chapter starts with a breakdown of the more established paths within psychology. Unlike popular belief, an undergraduate degree in psychology does not qualify you to practise as a professional psychologist and the information given in the first section will help you get a better sense of the postgraduate study requirements. In this chapter you will also find some useful guidelines on what you should consider when deciding what postgraduate study to pursue. Here we will discuss career options outside psychology and areas of interest for psychology graduates, whereas in later chapters you will find out more about popular areas to practise as a professional psychologist. To help you with your career preparation, opportunities and the importance of work experience will be explored in the final section.

Careers as a psychologist

As a psychology student, you will be able to choose from various established career paths according to your interests and the career direction you wish to follow. You will find though that most, if not all, specialised areas require you to complete further study in the form of a postgraduate training programme. Table 7.1 below offers a brief description of the type of work involved in the nine areas of psychology in which it is possible to become a chartered psychologist. As with most professions, attaining chartered status is no simple task and becoming a chartered psychologist is no exception to the rule. To achieve this there are certain steps to take (see also Chapter 2):

- First, you will need to gain Graduate Basis of Chartered Membership (GBC) with BPS (see Chapter 2).

- Second, you will need to register with the Health and Care Professions Council (HCPC). Recent changes in regulatory bodies mean that seven out of the nine psychology areas are now regulated by the HCPC. Hence, if you are intending to work as a professional psychologist you will need to register with the HCPC.

Table 7.1 will give you a better idea of the qualification and experience required to practise as a psychologist in each of the nine specialised paths. By satisfying these requirements you will be able to gain chartership with the BPS and have the opportunity to register with the HCPC.

Career choice	Description of type of work	Qualification needed
Clinical psychologist	Clinical psychologists work largely in health and social care settings including hospitals, health centres, community mental health teams, child and adolescent mental health services and social services. They assess clients using psychometric tests, interviews and direct observations which may lead to therapy or counselling.	Complete a Doctorate in Clinical Psychology (or equivalent) that has been approved by the HCPC. Read more about training as a clinical psychologist in Chapter 8.
Counselling psychologist	Counselling psychologists work almost anywhere there are people. For instance, counselling psychologists are currently employed in industry, commerce, the prison service and in all layers of education from primary school to university. Counselling psychologists can be self employed and also work in commerce as organisational consultants.	Complete a three-year full-time Doctorate in Counselling Psychology (or equivalent) that has been approved by the HCPC. Read more about training as a counselling psychologist in Chapter 9.

Career choice	Description of type of work	Qualification needed
Educational psychologist	Education psychologists work in schools, colleges, nurseries and special units, primarily with teachers and parents. A growing number also work as independent or private consultants. Their work can be directly with a child (assessing progress, giving counselling) or indirectly (through their work with parents, teachers and other professionals).	Complete a Doctorate in Educational Psychology (or equivalent) that has been approved by the HCPC. Read more about training as a educational psychologist in Chapter 12.
Forensic psychologist	Forensic psychologists specialise in criminal profiling, but also design and deliver treatment programmes, provide advice on public policy and new laws and help assess the psychological state of criminals. They are primarily employed by the HM Prison Service. Forensic psychologists can also be employed in the health service (including rehabilitation units and secure hospitals), the social service and work as independent consultants.	Complete an MSc in Forensic Psychology and Stage 2 of the Society's Diploma that has been approved by the HCPC. Alternatively, complete a Doctorate in Forensic Psychology. Read more about training as a forensic psychologist in Chapter 11.

Career choice	Description of type of work	Qualification needed
Neuro-psychologist	Neuropsychologists work with people of all ages with neurological problems, which might include traumatic brain injury, stroke, toxic and metabolic disorders, tumours and neurodegenerative diseases. Neuropsychologists require not only general clinical skills and knowledge of the broad range of mental health problems, but also a substantial degree of specialist knowledge in the neurosciences. Specialist skills are required in the assessment of neurological patients and rehabilitation encompasses a broad range of specialist behavioural and cognitive interventions, not only for the client but also for the client's family and carers.	Complete an accredited postgraduate training programme accredited by the BPS through the Clinical or Educational training route.

Alternatively you can complete the Society's Qualification in Clinical Neuropsychology (QiCN) which gives eligibility for entry onto the Society's Specialist Register of Clinical Neuropsychologists. |
| **Health psychologist** | Health psychologists are represented in a number of settings, such as hospitals, academic health research units, health authorities and university departments. They may deal with problems identified by healthcare agencies, including NHS Trusts and health authorities and health professionals such as GPs and nurses. However some new areas of work include health promotion and prevention of 'lifestyle' diseases, whereas rehabilitation is another growing area for health psychologists. | Complete a BPS accredited Master's in Health Psychology and Stage 2 Qualification in Health Psychology.

Alternatively you can complete a Doctorate in Health Psychology that is approved by the HCPC. |

Career choice	Description of type of work	Qualification needed
Occupational psychologist	Occupational psychologists are interested in helping organisations maximise performance of employees by looking at how people operate in the workplace. Their work is varied and involves working alongside other professionals such as managers, trade union representatives, training offices and specialist staff from the firm or industry concerned. The Civil Service is one of the largest single employers of occupational psychologists. A growing number of occupational psychologists are self-employed.	Complete a postgraduate qualification in Occupational Psychology that is BPS accredited and Stage 2 Qualification in Occupational Psychology. Read more about training as an occupational psychologist in Chapter 10.
Sport and exercise psychologist	Sport and exercise psychologists are interested in helping athletes psychologically prepare to compete and deal with the demands of training. Sport psychologists provide counselling to referees, they advise coaches, and help athletes overcome emotional problems resulting from injuries. Exercise psychologists concentrate on applying psychology to motivate people to exercise. Some sports psychologists hold positions with professional sports teams or national governing bodies, however most combine consultancy work with teaching and research. Exercise psychologists also combine consultancy work with teaching and research.	Complete a BPS accredited Master's in Sport and Exercise Psychology and stage 2 Qualification in Sport and Exercise Psychology.

Career choice	Description of type of work	Qualification needed
Teaching psychology	Teaching and research in psychology usually go hand in hand. Some teaching staff will have qualified in one of the applied psychological areas. They may return to teaching to develop professional practice, share knowledge and conduct research. Schools and colleges now offer psycho-logy as a subject at GCSE, A level, A/S level and as part of a general studies programme. Teachers prepare students for published syllabuses set by the examining bodies, so their work is not as flexible as that of teachers of undergraduates. Nevertheless, there is considerable choice in what to offer within the syllabus and an enormous range of possible studies in practical and laboratory courses.	Complete a BPS accredited degree, followed by a postgraduate qualification in your area of interest and five or more years supervised and assessed professional activity. Complete a PhD to follow the research route. If you wish to teach at schools or colleges you may be required to complete a Postgraduate Certificate in Education (PGCE).

Table 7.1: Description of nine specialised psychology paths and qualifications needed to practise them. (Adapted from BPS, 2012)

How to choose the right postgraduate course

There are several elements you ought to consider when choosing a postgraduate course. This is a simple three step guide to help you start your research:

Step 1 – Decide on the subject area

You will find that depending on the area you choose the length of postgraduate training programmes vary; typically becoming a

BPP
LEARNING MEDIA

psychologist practitioner requires three years of further study. However there are some specialisations, eg clinical psychology, that may take you longer to complete.

Step 2 – Check accreditation of the course and reputation of the institution

If you are looking to complete a postgraduate training programme as a step towards becoming a chartered psychologist then it would be advisable to visit the BPS website to search for postgraduate courses that are accredited by the Society. The completion of an accredited training programme will enable you to gain membership in the respective specialist group of the Society. Since 2009, seven out of the nine specialist areas in psychology have been regulated by the HCPC. To make sure that you do opt for a course that will allow you to register with the HCPC, cross check that it has indeed been approved by visiting the HCPC website (see Useful resources at the end of this chapter).

Once you have confirmed that the postgraduate course you have chosen fulfils the above requirements it would be advisable to check as well the reputation of the course / institution. You can visit the Quality Assurance Agency for Higher Education (QAA) website (www.qaa. ac.uk) for quality reports on higher education institutions, and also look at the university guide subject tables such as the Complete University Guide (see Useful resources) to find out more about students' career destinations, the research activity of the psychology departments, and more specifically the research conducted in the area you wish to specialise in. If you are currently studying at undergraduate level, it would be useful to speak to your tutors as they may have knowledge and personal contacts relating to their subject area that can point you to suitable postgraduate courses.

Step 3 – Check entry requirements and funding options

In terms of entry requirements, competition for postgraduate places can be tough in psychology, particularly for places in clinical programmes. Academic entry requirements for most postgraduate courses in psychology will expect you to have graduated with a good honours degree. However for certain programmes this may well not be sufficient and relevant work experience is required. As for funding options, these will vary between specialisations. Apart from clinical training that is funded by the NHS, other types of postgraduate study are quite often self-funded by students. In this respect, it is always useful to explore whether the university or psychology department you will be studying in offers scholarships, bursaries or a grants you can apply for (see the section on 'Other sources of funding' in Chapter 5).

Top tip

- Make sure to check university ranking before applying
- Review the content of the course and whether it matches your needs and job aspirations
- Consider the reputation of the department
- Find out about the quality of teaching

What other career options are available to psychology graduates?

Although many psychology students enter university intending to become professional psychologists, only about 20% go on to do this (Lantz, 2011). What this means is that a large percentage of students will find jobs in other areas; a 2010 Higher Education Statistics Agency (HESA) survey of 2009 graduates indicated that psychology graduates entered into a wide range of jobs in a variety of sectors. More specifically, of those who entered graduate-level jobs:

- 16% of graduates entered social and welfare occupations.

- 7% of graduates went into management roles in various sectors including retail, banking and marketing.

- 4% of graduates pursued work in business and finance industries.

Other psychology graduates pursued careers in sales and advertising; the health professions; education; IT; arts, design, culture and sports; engineering; scientific research; and other unspecified occupations.

Hence, one of the main benefits of studying a psychology degree is that the skills you acquire are widely applicable and will allow you to pursue careers in a variety of fields. In this respect it would be useful to investigate your wider career options, starting perhaps from the ones that are more closely related to your degree. There are several emerging areas of psychology that non professional psychologists can work in, including amongst others, coaching psychology, environmental psychology, marketing and consumer psychology, animal and pet psychology and human computer interaction (HCI). It would be advisable to look into these career paths in more detail, as some will still involve completing a postgraduate qualification. You can read more about these psychology related options in the *Psychology Student Employability Guide*, accessible via the Psychology Network archive (see Useful resources).

'I completed an undergraduate course in psychology followed by an MSc in Organisational Psychology and got my first graduate job as a Learning and Development Officer at a construction company. My work in L&D is diverse, I spend my days running behavioural training sessions for employees, analysing data from surveys and conducting one-to-one coaching sessions with managers. Although I don't work as a professional psychologist, this role has allowed me to apply the knowledge and skills acquired in my psychology degrees in a business context.'

As mentioned before, a large number of psychology graduates find employment in the health and social care fields. When conducting your research, it is worth exploring opportunities in the public, private and voluntary / third sector. Similarly to psychology related areas, some of the roles may require further training and experience for example, social worker, occupational therapist, mental health nurse. Also recently, new positions have emerged through the initiative of Improving Access to Psychological Therapies (IAPT) and are particularly suited to psychology graduates who are keen to work with mental health patients but are not interested in pursuing a doctoral level qualification. Some typical examples would include working as a psychological wellbeing practitioner (PWP) or a high intensity therapist (HIT). However if you are interested in the health sector, but don't necessarily want to work in a psychology-related role you can always look into the various management opportunities available in the NHS.

Finally in the event you decide to change career direction all together, the skills acquired in this arena will only help to broaden your choices. For instance, psychology graduates are often eligible to apply for management training schemes across a variety of industry sectors for example, retail, consultancy and banking. Some other examples of roles where your degree will be useful include becoming a careers advisor / career consultant, human resources officer, market researcher, public affairs consultant and editorial assistant. With all these roles you will find that work or volunteering experience will be helpful, if not essential in standing out from the crowd. Depending on your preferred path it may be worthwhile undertaking some further vocational study in order to increase your chances of being selected.

'During my third year I started investigating alternative career options and the careers service at my university advised me to look through the Prospects website for graduates. I was surprised to see that most graduate schemes were open to psychology graduates and was most attracted to the Civil Service Fast Stream. I felt that the skills gained in my degree helped me prepare for the rigorous assessment process which involved group exercises, written tests and an interview'.

The benefits of work experience

No doubt studying psychology allows you to develop a range of skills applicable to the world of work. However work experience is very important, now more than ever, in helping you get to grips with the mechanics of the job market and enabling you to explore career opportunities outside the psychology field. Whether you are looking to apply for psychology postgraduate study, or are in the process of investigating other career paths, work experience will be critical in your job hunt. Top UK employers report that half of their posts will be filled by individuals who already have work experience with their particular organisation. In particular if you are looking to enter a postgraduate programme of study, work experience is one of the main requirements. Take for example the clinical route where gaining experience as 'assistant psychologist' or 'research assistant' is almost imperative in securing a place on the clinical doctorate programme. (For more detail on clinical psychology see Chapter 8.) Visit the careers and education section on the BPS website (see Useful resources) for a list of useful websites to help you identify local volunteering opportunities.

Work experience is also beneficial in exploring psychology-related career paths. To this end, volunteering is an excellent way to make a positive contribution to society and also gain an insight into organisations you may wish to work for in the future. Take some time to think about what you've enjoyed in your degree and which psychology-related areas interest you the most and target your applications accordingly. As for how volunteering is viewed by employers, three-quarters of the Top 200 UK employers noted that they prefer to employ candidates with volunteer experience as this demonstrates their level of motivation (Lantz, 2011). Some useful resources include *The Guardian* volunteering jobs section and the Just Jobs 4 Students website (see the end of this chapter for more information).

Finally, if at some point you decide to move away from psychology and explore career paths in other sectors, internships can really improve your understanding of a particular job or industry. Depending on the sector and employer, internships can last anything from a few weeks during the summer holidays to a year. As an undergraduate student, you are more likely to be applying for placements run in the holiday period. Visit the graduate Prospects website for useful links (see end of chapter).

Case study

Katie studied psychology at the University of Manchester and gained a Doctorate in Clinical Psychology from University College London. Early on in her studies, Katie developed a passion for working with people with mental difficulties. Training as a clinical psychologist was her top career choice, but a very competitive one. Since she wasn't able to self-fund her studies, it was imperative for Katie to secure full funding for her training. After graduating she gained work experience as a healthcare assistant with the NHS. Katie also secured a post as a research assistant on a number of research projects. Both experiences gave her good grounding on what the role of a clinical psychologist involves and allowed her to work closely with clinical psychologists. Katie built a good relationship with her supervisors, who also endorsed her application for clinical training and played a decisive role in getting her a place on the programme.

Chapter summary

There are many options available to psychology graduates. Starting your job search early will allow you to explore different career paths and eventually decide on the right one for you. If you do decide to become a professional psychologist then make sure that you thoroughly investigate the academic and professional requirements and job opportunities available in your chosen area of specialisation. Don't forget that practising as a professional psychologist although rewarding will not suit everyone. Volunteering is always a great way for you to test the waters before committing to an area of work. It is also invaluable in showing your interest to potential employers and broadening your skill set.

Key points

- Research the areas of psychology in which you can work as a professional psychologist

- Identify the areas that interest you most and explore opportunities for gaining voluntary or paid work experience

- Consider all relevant elements before deciding on a postgraduate course

- Don't forget that you can use your psychology degree to move into other career fields

Useful resources

British Psychological Society: www.bps.org.uk

Just Jobs 4 Students website: www.justjobs4students.co.uk

Health and Care Profession Council: www.hcpc-uk.org

Prospects – graduate website: www.prospects.ac.uk

Psychology Network archive: www.pnarchive.org

The Complete University Guide: www.thecompleteuniversityguide.co.uk

The Quality Assurance Agency for Higher Education: www.qaa.ac.uk

References

BPS (2012) *How to become a psychologist* [Online] Available at: www.bps.org.uk/careers-education-training/how-become-psychologist/how-become-psychologist [Accessed 7 December 2012].

Lantz, C (2011) *Psychology Student: Employability Guide from University to Career.* [Online] The Higher Education Psychology Network. University of York. Available at: www.pnarchive.org/docs/pdf/EMPLOYABILITY_GUIDE.pdf [Accessed 10 February 2012].

Chapter 8

Becoming a clinical psychologist

Dr Rumina Taylor

So you're thinking about becoming a clinical psychologist? That's great to hear. This chapter explains the process by which one can become such a psychologist. It begins with a description of the field of clinical psychology and what roles clinical psychologists take within professional practice. We then move on to consider what qualities you need to become a clinical psychologist, which should help you to decide whether such a career is for you. If it is, the rest of the chapter explains the necessary steps you need to take. We will look at what you need to do after completing an undergraduate degree, the application process for clinical training, what different clinical courses have to offer, and how you can plan your finances before, during and after training. We'll conclude by looking at some of the career paths you can pursue after qualifying. There are also some helpful websites and resources listed at the end that you might want to check out.

Increasing numbers of people are completing a psychology degree at undergraduate level perhaps because the subject is interesting and the skills learnt easily transferable to a variety of graduate professions. This means there are many career options for those with psychology degrees outside the field such as in business, marketing, PR or human resources. Becoming a psychologist is just one career path.

Top tip

Becoming a practitioner psychologist does require further training in addition to an undergraduate degree, normally three years of extra study.

This chapter is only concerned with the route to becoming a clinical psychologist but you are encouraged to find out more about alternative roles within the field to ensure you choose the right career for you. Check out the BPS and National Health Service (NHS) websites (see Useful resources at the end of this chapter and Chapters 11 and 12) for more information about practitioner psychologist careers.

Top tip

Take a look at the Higher Education Academy, *Psychology Student Employability Guide* (Lantz, 2011) (see References at the end of this chapter). This provides an overview of traditional psychology careers as well as new emerging psychology routes and external but related fields.

What is clinical psychology?

Clinical psychology is concerned with the mental health of people across the age span, from young children to older adults including those with learning disabilities. The Division of Clinical Psychology (DCP), which is part of the BPS, suggests the aims of the profession are '*to reduce psychological distress and to enhance and promote psychological wellbeing by the systematic application of knowledge derived from psychological theory and data*' (Toogood, 2010).

What work do clinical psychologists do?

Clinical psychologists work with people who have physical and mental health needs to help them cope, reduce their suffering, and improve their lives. This can involve working with those who are experiencing anxiety, depression, psychosis, difficulty adjusting to a physical illness, addictions, relationship difficulties, neurological disorder or brain injury. They are based in a variety of outpatient and inpatient settings such as in GP surgeries, hospitals, child, adult or older adult community mental health teams, rehabilitation, forensic and learning disability services. Their roles require the ability to work with individuals, couples, families, carers, and groups, as well as other health professionals from within and outside the discipline.

> '*For as long as I can remember I have been interested in mental health and how people can show much resilience when faced with such difficulties. I guess I wanted to be a part of that and have the opportunity to help people feel better about themselves be it through carrying out research or providing therapy. It's really rewarding work.*'
> **Dr Helen Waller, Clinical Psychologist, Institute of Psychiatry, King's College London, South London and Maudsley NHS Foundation Trust**

Clinical psychologists assess clients using interviews, behavioural observation or more formal psychological and psychometric tests, which inform appropriate interventions such as the provision of therapy. They are referred to as scientist practitioners as they draw on psychological theory and research (known as the evidence base) to work out what is affecting a person's wellbeing and what is maintaining their distress. This process is often referred to as *formulation* and it guides the treatment of a client's difficulty. Therapeutic interventions once implemented are monitored and changed as necessary to ensure the client's needs continue to be met.

'The thing I love about clinical psychology is being able to use scientific knowledge, theory, analytical thinking and intuition to try to help understand and improve someone's experience within an (often intense) interpersonal relationship. A unique combination and a very privileged position to be in.'

The role of a clinical psychologist is varied and diverse and does not only involve the provision of therapy. Clinical psychologists carry out research often alongside their clinical jobs in order to contribute to the evidence base. They teach, supervise, and work with other psychologist colleagues and health professionals to provide psychological knowledge and to develop psychologically-informed ways of thinking (Toogood, 2010). They also take on leadership roles within their day-to-day work and an increasing number are involved in service planning, change, and delivery. Clinical psychologists work predominately within the NHS and some work in private practice too. A large number have links with universities where they carry out research and teaching.

What skills and interests do you need to become a clinical psychologist?

It's important to consider whether becoming a clinical psychologist is the right career for you. In addition to completing a second degree of a further three years, competition for training places is high. The application process can be tough and that's before you have even started the course.

Top tips

- Getting onto a training course requires persistence, determination, and a real interest to pursue the profession.

- The application stage is stressful and therefore it is important to ensure you have a network of support around you who can help you get through the process. Some candidates also find forums a helpful source of support (see Useful resources at the end of this chapter).

- It's important to consider what you want out of a career and whether clinical psychology can satisfy you. Ultimately, would you enjoy being a clinical psychologist?

- How would listening to other people's difficulties and containing their distress on a day-to-day basis be for you? Would you be ok?

There are certain skills, qualities and interests that are likely to make you a good clinical psychologist and lead you to have a fulfilling and rewarding career. If you are intrigued to find out why people think, feel, and behave the way they do then the profession may be for you. Being a good therapist requires active and analytical listening skills, as well as the ability to have empathy and warmth for others. It is important to consider the impact working with those with mental health needs would have on you.

The role often includes much contact with other health professionals so you have to engage in working as part of a team and have the necessary communication and negotiation skills. An interest in science and psychological theory is also needed, as this knowledge is what clinical psychologists refer to when trying to understand their clients' difficulties. Further, keeping up to date with research and the evidence base is crucial to ensure you continue to be a competent practitioner. Clinical psychology is a profession in which you are always learning and continuing to develop your strengths and work on your weaknesses. This can be exciting and motivating for some, but tiresome and stressful for others. Your role as a clinical psychologist will change over time as you take on more senior positions. As clinicians climb the profession ladder they are expected to take on more managerial and supervisory responsibility, which can mean a smaller caseload of clients to see.

Assess your skills: Key skills and interests

- A genuine interest in helping others with their emotional needs by working with them collaboratively to solve difficulties

- Effective communication, negotiation, and listening skills

- The ability to work as part of a team

- An interest in psychological science and the drive to keep up to date with new developments and findings

- The ability to work within a profession that emphasises continued professional development with possible job role changes along the way

How do you become a clinical psychologist?

We have already emphasised the importance of BPS accreditation and in order to apply for a clinical psychology course you need to have GBC with BPS (see Chapter 2).

Once you have achieved GBC you are then in the position to apply for a postgraduate degree and train as a clinical psychologist. The course consists of a three-year full-time Doctorate in Clinical Psychology, the only exception being the University of Edinburgh in Scotland which offers a specialist training package consisting of part-time training and part-time working over four to five years. Trainees spend at least half of their training working with people from across the age span who are experiencing psychological distress. Clinical practice is assessed by placement supervisors and typically via written case reports over the course of training. Other time is spent in academic teaching such as in lectures, workshops, seminars and tutorials. Performance can be assessed using a variety of methods that differ depending on the course but can include: written exams, essays, and / or oral presentations. Trainees are also expected to carry out and submit a research thesis at the end of their training usually comprising a major research project and a smaller service-evaluation project.

Top tips

- Although eligibility for GBC requires a minimum 2.2 degree, clinical training courses will not normally accept candidates with a 2.2 unless they have completed an additional higher qualification such as a master's degree.

- All courses include clinical practice, academic work, and research. Trainees need to show competence in all three areas.

Similar to undergraduate degrees and conversion courses, clinical training programmes are also regulated and accredited. The BPS used to be responsible for formally accrediting courses but this has now changed. Since 2009 the Health and Care Professions Council (HCPC) has become the regulator for applied psychologists and is responsible for approving clinical training programmes. The HCPC keep a register of all health practitioners who meet their standards in terms of the training they received and their professional skills to ensure people receive appropriate care across a range of disciplines. You can visit the HCPC website (see Useful resources at the end of this chapter) to find out more about their role and to view the list of approved clinical training programmes.

Top tip

In order to use the title clinical psychologist you need to register with the HCPC after you have finished training. This also means you need to complete a Doctorate in Clinical Psychology course that has been approved by the HCPC.

The BPS continues to accredit clinical training courses although completion of a BPS accredited programme is not required to practise as a clinical psychologist. However, if your training is accredited then this confers eligibility for chartered psychologist status with the BPS. This is a widely known and highly valued professional recognition, which highlights your competence and expertise as a psychologist. Visit the BPS website's membership section (see Useful resources at the end of this chapter) to find out more about becoming a chartered psychologist.

Previous experience

Currently (2012 intake), there are 32 clinical psychology training programmes and all are both HCPC approved and BPS accredited. Courses span the entirety of the UK and different courses have a different number of applicant places, ranging from seven to 40. Applications for clinical training are made online through the Clearing House, an educational charity based at the University of Leeds. This is with the exception of the University of Hull and Queen's University Belfast who have their own application process. Achieving a place on a training course is competitive and the Clearing House reports the success rate for the 2011 cohort to be at 16%, with only one in six applicants gaining a place.

Very few courses accept people immediately after completing an undergraduate degree and graduates require further clinical experience before applying. The most favourable positions are those as an assistant psychologist and / or research assistant. These posts provide candidates with the opportunity to work alongside and be supervised by a clinical psychologist. These roles, despite being competitive to attain, are very beneficial in demonstrating what it is like to work as a qualified clinical psychologist so candidates can make an informed decision before applying for the course. Many graduates work initially on a voluntary basis to gain enough experience in order to apply for such posts. Some candidates with an interest in the profession gain experience during their undergraduate degree by volunteering during term time or by finding appropriate work experience over the summer holidays. Other paid positions that allow you to work with those with mental health needs also count towards an application for clinical

training and can help in attaining an assistant post, for example as a healthcare assistant or social worker. However, some courses prefer candidates to have gained some clinical experience specifically under the supervision of a qualified clinical psychologist.

Top tips

In order to apply for clinical training you need:

- An undergraduate or conversion course which provides you with GBC

- An additional higher qualification such as a master's degree if you achieved a 2.2 or less in your undergraduate degree

- Some relevant clinical experience usually between one and three years (Toogood, 2010), and preferably as an assistant psychologist or research assistant under the supervision of a qualified clinical psychologist

Assistant psychologist and other relevant jobs tend to be advertised on the NHS jobs website (see Useful resources at the end of this chapter) although you could also look at your local NHS Trusts' website. The Clearing House also suggests useful websites (see the end of this chapter). Universities offering research assistant / worker roles often advertise these on their own websites under vacancies or on specific websites (see Useful resources).

Top tips

- If you are unsure whether the profession is for you then getting some work experience would be a good idea. If you can spend some time observing a clinical psychologist or even working with those who have mental health needs then you will gain an insight into what a career in clinical psychology would be like and whether it's for you.

- Some candidates gain experience during their undergraduate degree by volunteering during term time, for example at their university's Nightline service or by finding appropriate work experience over the summer.

- Contacting university career advisors, local hospitals, nursing homes, charities, and social services can be a useful place to start.

- The BPS lists a number of helpful websites (see Useful resources at the end of this chapter).

The application process

Once you have gained some clinically relevant experience and made the decision to pursue a career in clinical psychology, you are then in the position to apply for a clinical course. You don't need to have gained experience in every field clinical psychology has to offer before applying for training. University courses are more interested in the knowledge and skills you have acquired through your experiences and what you make of these both personally and professionally, rather than the numbers of years you have been working.

Application forms are made available each year on the Clearing House website at the start of September and need to be submitted by the start of December in order to be considered for a course starting the following autumn.

Step 1: Completing the application form

The application form is six pages long and starts by asking for your personal contact details and then which four courses you want to apply for. Applicants are also requested to provide two referees, one that can comment on academic ability and another who can describe relevant experience. The Clearing House requests academic transcripts for undergraduate, postgraduate or conversion courses are sent with the application form as proof of GBC and academic ability. If you have completed your degree outside the UK but have GBC, they ask for a letter confirming this from the BPS. The next bit of the form requires you to list your qualifications from school and university and to briefly describe your current and previous occupational and research experience.

The remainder of the form asks you to explain how you think your experiences to date have made you a better candidate for clinical training and what you hope to get out of training. There are also sections for you to describe more personal information about yourself, such as your interests outside of the profession and an opportunity to list your publications if you have any. The application form is followed by an equal opportunities monitoring form, which asks about a candidate's age, gender, marital status etc. This data is not used in the selection process and is anonymised. The Clearing House explains that the purpose for this data collection is to monitor whether those who apply for training are representative of the general population and also to ensure that the way courses choose their applicants does not involve any form of discrimination. Once you have completed your application it can be submitted through the Clearing House online system. At this stage the Clearing House will also ask you to pay a registration fee (currently £25) in order to process your form and send it to the courses you have selected.

'The hardest thing about the application form was the limited space! I found I had so much I wanted to say but instead had to spend a lot of time reflecting on my experiences. This helped me get down on paper the knowledge and skills I had learnt and clarified why I wanted to put myself through another three years of demanding study! Lots of people say it's tough to get on a training course so I certainly felt the pressure from the start. It did take me a few goes to get a place and although that was disappointing at the time, I do feel those extra years of work experience have helped me now I'm on the course. The leap from assistant psychologist to clinical trainee has felt less overwhelming and I have continued to draw on my previous experience, which has been advantageous for some clinical placements.'

Step 2: Choosing a clinical training course

There are 32 clinical training programmes that span the entirety of the UK and which courses you choose could depend on a number of factors. Location may be an important consideration. You may not want to move from where you are currently living so your choice of clinical course may be restricted to those local to you. On the other hand moving location may be something you want to do. Individual training programmes also differ from one another in terms of their structure and focus. For example, some courses have expertise in particular therapeutic approaches (eg Salomons, Canterbury Christ Church University: psychodynamic psychotherapy; Institute of Psychiatry, King's College London: cognitive behavioural approaches) and therefore training is more concentrated around these although other psychological models are covered. This may suit you very well if your interests also lie in these particular therapies. Other courses offer a more eclectic mix. Clinical placements also differ from course to course. Some courses offer six-month placements whereas others prefer their trainees to compete year-long placements. In addition, some clinical programmes cover a wide geographical area so some travelling to placements may be required. However, courses usually reimburse travelling to placement costs. Each course centre has provided detailed information about their programme on the Clearing House website (see Useful resources at the end of this chapter) where they describe their course structure, content and focus, as well as the geographical area covered, entry requirements and selection procedure. The DCP prequalification group also publishes the *Alternative Handbook* every year, which comprises the views of current clinical psychology trainees from all courses (see Useful resources).

Step 3: The interview process

Course centres normally inform you of the outcome of your application by the middle of March. Some courses request applicants to sit a written test before they shortlist for interview so may contact candidates earlier. Interviews are held between March and June in which applicants are asked about their clinical experience, academic knowledge and research skills. This may take place in the form of one or two interviews and some courses include a written exercise or group task. Interview panels are interested in how you reflect on your experiences and are looking for a realistic understanding of the profession and the role of a clinical psychologist within the NHS. Courses will inform you as to whether you have successfully secured a place for training shortly after the interview. Courses may offer you a reserve place for interview or for training. This means that you are on a waiting list and dependent on other candidates declining an offer for interview or turning down a training place. Some candidates do receive more than one offer for interview or multiple training places and therefore other applicants do move up the reserve list as others accept interviews and places on their preferred course. If you are unsuccessful at gaining a place try not to be disheartened. You can apply again and most courses offer feedback after interview and some will provide feedback on your application form if you are not shortlisted for interview. Often candidates do not get offered interviews first time around and many do have to try more than once before they secure a place.

Case study

'My interest in psychology started after attending a talk during sixth form which was given by a research scientist. Her speciality wasn't psychology but in her talk she touched on human behaviour and on how two people can respond and act quite differently to very similar events. I remember being intrigued by this and lots of questions came to my mind in particular why this was the case. After finding out more about the subject, I went on to study psychology at the University of Aberdeen. Towards the end of my degree I sought advice from lecturers, tutors, and the university careers service about what my options would be after completing a psychology degree. I wanted to stay within the profession and was interested in both organisational and clinical psychology. I tried to gain as much knowledge and experience in these areas as I could. I took advantage of the lectures available in these fields, selecting relevant modules to take where I could. I also joined the university's Niteline service which provided excellent training in listening and communication skills and showed me I could contain another person's distress. My thesis investigated

stress in the workplace and collecting data allowed me to be part of a busy city workforce providing me with first hand experience of the psychological processes that occur. I also volunteered during my summer holidays and with some nagging was able to gain work experience as a befriender on an older adult's ward and in a learning disabilities community service. These experiences confirmed my preference for clinical psychology and once I graduated I applied for assistant psychologist and research assistant posts. It did take me some months to get an assistant post but eventually I was offered a job. The clinical work I did was part of a research trial being carried out so it gave me the opportunity to gain not only clinical but also research experience.

I did not apply for clinical training immediately and spent some time gaining knowledge and skills to talk about on my form. When I did apply I was lucky to be offered interviews. I found the interviews challenging and the first one did not go as well as I hoped! However, it gave me a real insight into what course tutors were looking for and it forced me to really think about the profession, what I had learnt from my experiences, and what I could contribute to the field. In the end I was offered a place and completed my clinical training at the Institute of Psychiatry, Kings College London. I thoroughly enjoyed my training although it was hard work and a steep learning curve at times! Since qualifying I have continued to work with those with psychosis and longer term mental health needs and my role involves clinical, teaching, and research. I enjoy the multi-faceted nature of my role as a clinical psychologist and never seem to get bored!'

Planning your finances

Training as a clinical psychologist is funded through the NHS. This means that when you start a training course you are employed as a trainee clinical psychologist and receive a salary from the NHS. Trainees are paid at band six with a minimum salary of £25,528 per year and qualified clinical psychologists start from band seven with a minimum salary of £30,460 per year (April 2011 figures). Staff who work in high cost areas such as London also receive extra pay on top of this basic salary. In the past it has not been possible to pay for a place on training as funding has always been provided by the NHS. However, this appears to be changing with a small number of self-funded places becoming available on certain courses. The Clearing House provides information about fee-paying places that are available on courses. Assistant psychologists are normally placed between bands four to six

on the NHS pay scales. For the most recent salary information please look at the NHS careers website (see Useful resources at the end of this chapter).

Research assistants are usually employed by universities and therefore do not normally receive pay from the NHS. Universities typically have their own pay scales, which are often similar to the NHS. In the past research workers have been known to receive a slightly higher salary compared to assistant psychologists although this depends on the nature of their role and the specific university.

Your career as a clinical psychologist

Newly qualified clinical psychologists often take up posts in the NHS, although some may move into the private sector or see private clients in addition to their roles within the NHS. Which area of clinical psychology you pursue will largely depend on your interests and what jobs are available at the time of qualifying. Clinical courses provide clinical and research experience, which allows trainees to realise where their skills and interests lie. This can make choosing which jobs to apply for after training easier. You could take up a post working with children, adolescents, adults, older adults or with those with physical health problems, brain injury or learning disabilities. Some clinical psychologists go onto specialise in their area of interest and complete additional diplomas or masters' degrees to enhance their knowledge and gain further accreditations. Others follow a teaching and research path taking up posts within universities. This route can often include completing a research PhD. Whichever path you choose the profession is rewarding, fulfilling, and enjoyable.

Chapter summary

This chapter has explained the route to becoming a clinical psychologist. We have looked at the roles clinical psychologists take in practice and the qualities and interests required for the profession. The steps from undergraduate level to attaining a place on a clinical course have also been described. This chapter has provided you with a realistic overview of the profession and the pathway to becoming a qualified clinical psychologist, as well as highlighting important issues that need consideration. If you have decided to pursue the profession good luck in the exciting and challenging journey ahead of you. Be persistent with the process and try not to feel frustrated if it takes you longer than you initially hoped to achieve a place on a clinical course. There is no rush to get a training place and the experience you gain before starting a course will stand you in good stead during and after training. Being a clinical psychologist is very rewarding and the diversity within the role makes it an interesting career.

Key points

- Clinical psychology is concerned with the mental health of people across the age span. The role of a clinical psychologist is varied and diverse and does not only involve the provision of therapy.

- It is important to consider whether becoming a clinical psychologist is the right career for you. Think about the impact working with those with mental health needs would have on you.

- Few courses accept people immediately after completing an undergraduate degree. Graduates require clinical experience before applying and an undergraduate or conversion course, which provides GBC.

- Application forms for clinical courses are made available each year on the Clearing House website at the start of September and need to be submitted by the start of December. Interviews are held between March and June in which applicants are asked about their clinical experience, academic knowledge and research skills.

- All courses include clinical practice, academic work, and research. Trainees need to show competence in all three areas.

- When candidates start a training course they are employed as a trainee clinical psychologist and receive a salary from the NHS.

- Newly qualified clinical psychologists often take up posts in the NHS. In order to use the title 'clinical psychologist', registering with the HCPC after completing training is necessary.

Useful resources

The British Psychological Society (BPS):
www.bps.org.uk

Careers section:
www.bps.org.uk/careers

Membership section:
www.bps.org.uk/what-we-do/benefits-belonging/membership/membership

Volunteering opportunities:
www.do-it.org.uk
www.timebank.org.uk
www.vinspired.com
www.volunteering.org.uk

Clearing House:
www.leeds.ac.uk/chpccp

Clinical training programmes:
www.leeds.ac.uk/chpccp/Course.html

Fee-paying places:
www.leeds.ac.uk/chpccp/BasicFunding.html

University of Hull:
www2.hull.ac.uk/pgmi/cmr/clinicalpsychology/information--doctorate.aspx

Queen's University Belfast
www.qub.ac.uk/schools/psy/StudyingAtTheSchool/PostgraduateTaught/DClinPsych/

Jobs:
www.jobsincharities.co.uk
www.charityjob.co.uk
www.psychminded.co.uk

Forums:
www.clinpsy.org.uk

The Division of Clinical Psychology (DCP):
http://dcp-prequal.bps.org.uk

Health and Care Professions Council (HCPC):
www.hcpc-uk.org

National Health Service (NHS):
www.nhscareers.nhs.uk

Jobs:
www.jobs.nhs.uk
www.nhscareers.nhs.uk/ahp.shtml

Research assistant jobs:
www.jobs.ac.uk

References

Lantz, C (2011) *Psychology Student Employability Guide from University to Career.* [Online] The Higher Education Academy Psychology Network. University of York. Available at: www.pnarchive.org/docs/pdf/EMPLOYABILITY_GUIDE.pdf [Accessed 02 July 2012].

Toogood, R (2010). *The Core Purpose and Philosophy of the Profession.* Division of Clinical Psychology, The British Psychological Society.

Chapter 9

Becoming a counselling psychologist

Dr Myrto Tsakopoulou

In recent years, counselling psychology has become one of the most popular choices of professional psychology. It is increasingly gaining respectability as an independent branch of psychology and it offers employability within a wide range of work settings. In this chapter you will get an overview of what counselling psychology is, how it differs from other types of 'talking therapy' and how you can train to become a counselling psychologist. We will look at what you will need in preparation for the training (entry requirements and previous experience), what the training involves and how to manage your finances.

What is counselling psychology?

Counselling psychology is a type of applied psychology that falls within the professional area of what is commonly known as 'talking therapy'. Counselling psychologists work with people with a variety of mental health problems such as depression and anxiety, people with relationship problems and people who may have to cope with difficult situations and experiences, such as the loss of a loved one or a traumatic accident. They help people to understand the psychological causes of their emotional difficulties, to realise the possibilities of change and to learn better ways of coping

Counselling psychology is a relatively new branch of professional psychology but it has its roots within the humanistic, existential, psychoanalytic and behavioural approaches that formed the science of psychology as a whole. It is the combined application of the humanistic nature of *counselling* and the science of *psychology*. Counselling is a predominantly humanistic approach to understanding a person's problem which theorises the skills of listening, empathising and placing the relationship between psychologist and client (the 'therapeutic relationship') in central focus towards psychological change. The person's difficulties are seen as individual and the psychologist's role is to work with the client towards the individual formulation or understanding of their problems, based on their unique, personal life experiences. The practitioner uses his or her reflective capacity to relate to the subjective experience of the client. Psychology is the more scientific way of understanding human behaviour. It is based on the notion that there are commonalities between individuals and that human behaviour can be measured, studied and theories can be drawn from its study.

Differences and similarities with clinical psychology, counselling and psychotherapy

Counselling psychology has a lot in common with clinical psychology but also with the practice of counselling and psychotherapy. All these professions are involved with similar client groups and the practice of psychological therapies. Clinical and counselling psychologists commonly identify more with the role of the 'scientist-practitioner', with an emphasis on practice that is based on research evidence rather than solely on the experiential knowledge of the practitioner and their theoretical approach. However, the differences between these professions are not clearly defined and they very much depend on the individual practitioner's interests, aspirations and work philosophy. Clinical and counselling psychology courses have very similar layouts (with emphasis both on clinical and research practice), length of study and overall qualifications (doctoral level). In terms of the differences between the two, they fall mainly within three areas:

- **Financial**: Clinical psychology training is funded by the NHS and trainees accepted on the course receive a salary throughout their training. Counselling psychology training is self-funded.

- **Placements**: Counselling psychology trainees have to find their own placements in order to practise their therapeutic skills, while clinical psychology trainees are allocated to relevant NHS services by their course.

- **Training**: Clinical psychologists train in administering neuropsychological and psychometric tests, such as intelligence, memory and personality tests. These are not routinely taught in counselling psychology courses but trainees may be given this opportunity within their training placements.

You do not have to hold a psychology degree to practise as a counsellor or psychotherapist and these professions have different training routes and accreditation process to counselling psychology. There are also some differences between them in terms of career options, as there seem to be more counselling psychology positions in statutory services like the NHS, while counsellors and psychotherapists generally work more in private practice or voluntary organisations.

Is it the right career for you?

Working as a counselling psychologist can be emotionally demanding but also very rewarding. The challenges begin with the training, which is costly and requires many hours of hard work, studying, attending lectures, finding suitable placements to practise therapeutic skills and coping with the emotional demands of the profession.

As a counselling psychologist you need to be able not only to listen carefully and to understand things from the other person's perspective, but also to be reflective of your own behaviour and emotions while you listen. You have to have the curiosity to learn from each individual that you work with and the ability to apply theory into practice. Counselling psychologists sometimes work with distressed people who have been through very difficult life experiences. You have to be able to listen to their life stories and to develop a trusting therapeutic relationship with them, which will help them learn better ways of coping. You may also have to work in challenging environments, such as hospitals or prisons. The reward for these challenges is to see people feel more in control of their feelings and their behaviour. The change is usually slow and not always obvious but you will be part of a person's journey in making sense of their experiences and their path towards a better life.

Many counselling psychologists also work privately, which means that they set up their own practice and are not part of a service, organisation or company. This gives you the freedom to choose your working hours, the type of client problems you feel more comfortable working with and to have more flexibility in your work. However, this can sometimes feel isolating as you are not part of a team and you also have the sole responsibility for the practicalities of your work, ie advertising your work and administrative tasks, such as booking appointments, amongst other things. It is also worth noting that you may never have complete flexibility as you will always have a commitment to meeting your clients on a regular basis, which is usually weekly.

> 'My advice would be to think carefully before choosing counselling psychology as a career route. It is a long and demanding process on many levels and you have to plan well and be prepared financially and emotionally.'

Which course to choose

Once you have decided that this is the right career for you, you need to start planning your path towards qualification early. You will need to ensure you gain some relevant experience in the field before applying for courses and you will need to complete postgraduate studies that meet the criteria for professional registration.

Since 2009, in order to be able to practise with the protected title of 'counselling psychologist' you must meet the Health and Care Professions Council (HCPC) registration standards. This means that you must complete an HCPC approved counselling psychology course or

meet the other HCPC routes for registration (voluntary register transfer, grandparenting or international route). As highlighted in other chapters, you may also want to consider applying for a British Psychological Society (BPS) accredited course, which will allow you to apply for 'chartered psychologist' status. BPS accredited courses can be found on the BPS website (see Useful resources at the end of this chapter). You are not legally required to be registered with HCPC or BPS to work as a 'psychologist', but having these titles reflects on higher professional recognition and increases your employability. Also, you do not have to follow these routes of qualification in order to work therapeutically with people or to practise counselling. You may want to consider a career in counselling or psychotherapy and for these professions you will need to meet the registration criteria of their respective registration bodies or of associations that provide training and membership in specialised types of therapy (see Useful resources at the end of the chapter for the websites of different professional bodies).

When choosing a course you may also need to consider practical factors, such as proximity to work and placement settings or cost of living in the area. If you have a particular interest in research it is worth considering the university's research reputation and what projects are being undertaken there. Or if you are interested in a specific therapeutic approach you can choose a course based on the main therapeutic model taught. Most courses have cognitive behavioural therapy as their main approach because it has good empirical evidence across a variety of mental health problems and it is favoured by most statutory employers. However, different course providers have different therapeutic traditions, so it is worth doing a bit of research on what is on offer and what best suits your skills and interests before you decide. You don't want to find yourself training in a therapeutic approach that does not fit in with your stance and drop out after great cost!

Before training

Entry requirements

Similar to clinical psychology you have to hold a good undergraduate psychology degree (usually a 2.1 or a 2.2 with an additional master's degree) or BPS accredited conversion, a BPS Graduate Basis for Chartered Membership (GBC) and to have some relevant previous experience. If English is not your first language you may be required to provide evidence of your proficiency usually with a good International

English Language Testing System (IELTS) score. The specific entry requirements may vary slightly between courses and you will have to contact each course provider individually for more details.

Previous experience

If you are interested in working as a counselling psychologist you should consider gaining some experience of working within a mental health setting from early on. Having previous experience, either paid or voluntary, highly increases your chances of being accepted by a course and will help you decide if this is the right professional route for you. Look for supportive mental health roles within the voluntary, charity and non-profitable sector in positions that will help you learn or enhance your counselling and interpersonal skills (eg Samaritans, Childline, Relate, Mind). You can consider positions similar to those recommended to clinical psychology trainees (see previous chapter) but perhaps with more emphasis on positions that have to do with direct contact with clients and less with research. Improving Access to Psychological Therapies (IAPT) is a recent government initiative which offers such positions. Working as an IAPT Psychological Wellbeing Practitioner can offer you the opportunity to train in specific psychological therapies (mainly cognitive behavioural therapy) within a mental health setting. These jobs are advertised on the NHS jobs website (see Useful resources at the end of this chapter).

Some counselling psychology courses may require that you can evidence your counselling skills, so completing a basic counselling skills course prior to applying could also increase your chances of getting into the course. Visit the British Association for Counselling and Psychotherapy (BACP) website for more details on relevant counselling skills courses and experience (see Useful resources at the end of the chapter).

Personal development and self awareness are very important aspects in the practice of counselling psychology and you will have to receive personal therapy throughout your training. It may help to start receiving therapy before your training as this will demonstrate your commitment to personal development and it might give you an advantage in the application process.

Top tips on gaining working experience

- Volunteer for any support or counselling position you can think of: helplines, mentoring schemes, online support services.

- Use your existing network: do you know anyone who can offer you paid or unpaid work in a support role?

- Start applying for relevant jobs early.

- Think about any support work positions that will offer you direct client work, even if it does not involve counselling, eg support officer in housing associations for people with mental health problems, healthcare assistant for older people, rehabilitation worker for people with substance misuse problems.

- Sign up for relevant conferences and seminars and network with people you meet there.

- Find your local counselling and psychology services and write to the managers offering work on a voluntary basis or asking for the opportunity to shadow a qualified counselling psychologist. Tempt them with your skills: offer to help with audit, outcome measures or with putting together a list of resources.

The application process

Once you have chosen a suitable course you can apply to a university or to a course provider individually. The application process usually involves filling out an application form with an accompanying personal statement, where you describe how you meet their entry requirements. If your application is successful, you will be called for an interview, where you will have to demonstrate that you fulfil their criteria and expand on your clinical and research interest for the course. The interview process may sometimes involve an experiential part, such as a mock counselling session. As counselling psychology is increasingly gaining popularity as a professional career, so has competition for the training. You should ensure you fulfil the basic entry requirements and try to gather as much experience as possible before you apply. If you are not successful the first time, you will usually have the opportunity to re-apply the next year; don't be disheartened! Remember that gathering experience is very important in this profession, so you can keep on increasing your skills and knowledge before you start your training. Also, re-applying can be an indication of your determination to be a counselling psychologist.

What does the training involve?

Accredited and approved courses in counselling psychology usually require that you complete the following during your training:

- Self development: personal therapy by a qualified practitioner (usually 60–80 hours across the training period)

- Membership with the BPS Division of Counselling Psychology

- Keeping a journal and critical reflection notes on your personal development throughout your training

- Course work and training: case studies and process reports, attendance of other training, conferences and seminars relevant to your studies, a critical review and analysis of your progression as a trainee

- Client work: liability insurance and workplace indemnity insurance, 450 hours of counselling hours over the whole of your training, clinical placement reports to be completed by your placement supervisor, case notes and a critical review of your ongoing client work

- Supervision: to receive supervision by a qualified practitioner (usually a counselling psychologist) who will complete relevant documentation (eg record of your attendance and evaluation form), supervision notes and a critical review of your development as a supervisee

- A doctoral thesis

At the end of each year, you will submit a log with evidence of your personal and professional progress and how you meet the above required criteria throughout your training.

Training routes

There are two training routes to achieving counselling psychology chartership: the BPS Qualification in Counselling Psychology (also known as 'the independent route') or a Doctorate in Counselling Psychology.

BPS Qualification in Counselling Psychology

This is the independent route where you can gain the relevant experience and qualifications towards BPS Chartership and HCPC registration without completing a postgraduate course. It is a doctoral level award, as described by the Quality Assurance Agency (QAA).

If you choose this route you have to meet a number of competences, academic and practice-based, as set out by the BPS. You can choose a qualified Coordinator of Training who can support you and monitor your progress. You have to take responsibility to complete assignments, attend relevant training courses and find suitable placements but you have more flexibility in your learning and professional development than if you undertake the Doctorate route. You have to pay fees to the BPS for each part of the qualification process (eg enrolment, documentation and assessment) and for relevant independent seminars and lectures.

For this route you need to apply directly through BPS. At the end of this chapter, you can find the websites that will give you full details about this route at the BPS website as well as the BPS *Candidate Handbook*.

Doctorate in Counselling Psychology

In order to be able to apply for chartership through this training route you have to have GBC and to complete a BPS accredited doctorate in counselling psychology. There are currently 12 such accredited courses (most of them based in London; see the end of this chapter for the website). The application process for these is similar to other postgraduate university courses. Once you have identified which university you would like to apply to and you have ensured that you meet their entry requirements, you will initially be required to fill out their application form. If you are successful at this stage, you will be invited for an interview, where you will have to demonstrate your relevant knowledge, skills and experience.

This is usually a three-year full-time doctoral course, which consists of theoretical, research and practice-based modules. You will have to attend lectures, seminars and supervision as outlined by the course. You may have to sit exams and you will have to submit assignments and yearly logs where you demonstrate your development throughout the course.

Planning your finances

Counselling psychology training can be very demanding financially. As it is self-funded you have to have enough money to cover your training needs (eg course fees) and you also have to cover your living costs (ie rent, food, transport). This can be challenging as a full-time training course does not allow enough time to keep a full-time job. For example, the doctorate course usually requires university attendance two to three times per week and you will have to allocate time for your practice placement and for studying. Some part-time courses and the more flexible independent route may allow you more time to maintain

paid employment. Or you may want to consider employment within a service that could also offer you access to client work, which can count towards your course's requirements (eg assistant psychologist and IAPT positions).

The fees for a three-year full-time doctorate course ranged between £6,800 to around £7,100 per year in 2011. You will need to check annual fees with each university individually. For the independent route you will have to pay for each part of your training process separately and you can find more information in the BPS Schedule of Fees (see the end of this chapter).

Your career as a counselling psychologist

Counselling psychologists can work in a wide range of settings, such as hospitals, schools, prisons and commercial organisations. They are employed within the statutory (eg NHS, social services), voluntary and private sectors, or they can be self-employed, running their own therapy practice or consultancy service. They can provide therapy, teaching, research and consultancy, depending on their career interests and abilities. They can work with individuals, couples, groups or families across the lifespan.

A counselling psychologist's salary starts at band seven of the NHS scale (in 2011 figures this is £30,460 pa) and they can work towards Consultant level at band nine (up to £100,000 pa). Working privately they can earn between £50–£150 per hour.

Case study

'My dream had always been to work therapeutically with people. I was always a good listener and I loved 'analysing' things. As a teenager when I thought of psychologists I thought of a deep thinker like Freud telling his patients things about themselves that they were not aware of and I loved literature portraying the complexities of the human mind and relationships such as Hermann Hesse and Franz Kafka. I wanted to understand why people thought and behaved the way they did.

However, deciding which professional route to take towards my goal was not an easy one. Clinical psychology seemed to have the appropriate kudos and you get paid for your training! But I found it a bit too 'prescriptive' and medically oriented. Psychotherapy and counselling were closer to my idea of therapy but they seemed

BPP LEARNING MEDIA

limited in their professional prospects. Counselling psychology had the perfect combination of all the elements I was looking for.

Becoming a counselling psychologist was a long and hard process. I was lucky to have part of my fees funded by my family and part funded by money I saved up working between my studies. It also helped that I always had a clear focus of what I wanted to achieve. Having a clear direction meant that I chose placements and jobs that would give me the skills and experience that I needed: I volunteered in psychiatric hospitals, I worked as a support worker in a mental health hostel and I gained counselling experience in a psychotherapy service. As a counselling psychology trainee no two days were the same in a week: Monday at the university, Tuesday at work, Wednesday placement, Thursday study day, Friday working on my research thesis. Varied and never boring but extremely demanding at times. You have to remain focused and to be prepared to have no life for a few years until you finish your studies. But when it's all over you will experience possibly one of the biggest achievements of your life.

When I tell people I have a doctorate they often say: "you must be clever!". But the truth is that it has little to do with intelligence. It's patience and perseverance you need the most.'

Chapter summary

Becoming a professional counselling psychologist is a demanding but rewarding process. With a good psychology undergraduate degree and relevant previous experience you can apply for further postgraduate training in counselling psychology. This is self-funded, usually lasts three years full-time and is of doctoral level. It involves training in psychological therapy and it will give you qualifications to work within the statutory, voluntary or private sectors with people with mental health problems or in emotional distress. It can be a challenging training experience as you will need to be equally proficient at research and counselling-oriented aspects of training.

Key points

- Counselling psychology is a branch of professional psychology that involves the application of psychological therapy in a wide variety of settings.

- To qualify as a counselling psychologist you will have to complete a professional doctorate or the BPS qualification in Counselling Psychology, which last usually three years if studied full-time and is self-funded.

- In order to be eligible to apply for the training you need to have a good degree in psychology and relevant previous experience in the form of a basic course counselling skills and / or relevant working experience.

- To be able to practise as a counselling psychologist you will need to fulfil the criteria of the HCPC and in order to maximise your employability you will need to fulfil the BPS criteria for chartership.

- As a qualified counselling psychologist you will be able to apply for jobs in the NHS, private and voluntary sector positions involving counselling skills or to set up your own private practice.

Useful resources

BPS accredited courses:
www.bps.org.uk

BPS Division of Counselling Psychology:
http://dcop.bps.org.uk/dcop/

BPS *Schedule of Fees*:
http://exams.bps.org.uk/exams/counselling-psychology/qcop.cfm

BPS Accredited Doctorate in Counselling Psychology courses:
www.bps.org.uk/careers-education-training/accredited-courses-
training-programmes/accredited-courses-training-progra

BPS Doctorate route to Counselling Psychology:
www.bps.org.uk/careers-education-training/society-qualifications/
society-qualifications

BPS *Doctorate Candidate Handbook*:
http://exams.bps.org.uk/exams/counselling-psychology/qcop.cfm

British Association for Counselling and Psychotherapy:
www.bacp.co.uk/

Health and Care Professions Council (HCPC):
www.hcpc-uk.org

UK Council for Psychotherapy:
www.psychotherapy.org.uk/

Other associations providing training and membership in specialised
types of therapy include:
www.babcp.com for cognitive behavioural therapy
www.bap-psychotherapy.org for psychoanalysis

Other websites providing information on counselling psychology
career opportunities:
www.jobs.nhs.uk
www.nhscareers.nhs.uk/
www.psychology.about.com/od/psychologycareerprofiles/p/
counseling-psychology.htm
www.iapt.nhs.uk

Chapter 10

Becoming an occupational (or organisational) psychologist

Robert Goate

'There are three things in life that people generally refuse to admit they are bad at: driving, making love and conducting an interview.'
(Jeff Grout – UK Managing Director of Robert Half International, specialist recruitment consultancy)

What is occupational psychology?

Occupational psychology is the science of people at work. Occupational psychologists apply psychological knowledge, theory and practice to work settings, with the aim of helping companies to improve the performance of their employees and its processes in order to make the organisation more successful. Occupational psychologists may work with individuals, teams or entire organisations.

Some occupational psychologists work in a consultancy role, while others work in-house in collaboration with management, human resources, recruitment, training, in fact any role where the human dimension of the company can benefit from their insight. Some occupational psychologists will use this title while working for, or in, organisations, however, there are many individuals who work within companies who will use other titles instead eg HR director / manager / specialist, business psychologist, business coach, performance manager, or reward specialist to identify themselves.

The key areas where occupational psychologist work are:

*   **Assessment, selection and talent development and management.** This will include designing, developing, evaluating and implementing selection procedures, including the administration of psychometric tests, assessment centre exercises and structured interviews. It also includes designing and administering development centres and follow up interventions

*   **Organisational change.** This includes diagnosing the current state of an organisation and proposing recommendations to aid the organisation as it goes through a change process. This may include running surveys on culture or engagement, and the analysis and integration of data into practical recommendations that will help the organisation achieve its outcomes. It can also include advising on new technologies or developments such as e-learning and social media, flexible shift patterns or virtual team working.

*   **Leadership.** This can include the use of psychometrics to aid the leader in identifying potential areas for development which can be addressed using coaching and mentoring initiatives.

- **Health and wellbeing**. This can include carrying out risk assessments, or a diagnosis of current working conditions from a health and safety perspective. It can also include recommendations to an organisation on implementing recent changes in legislation for example in the area of work-life balance and stress, or suggestions for the introduction of benefits or reward plans for employees.

- **Employee attitudes and motivation**. This includes carrying out surveys, interviews and analysis to establish how employees at an organisation think, feel and act while at work currently, and to propose evidence-based recommendations on what may improve their performance in future. This may include job redesign and communication skills.

- **Workplace design and ergonomics**. This includes working with engineers and health specialists to improve the design of the working environment and its equipment to make the workplace a happier, healthier, more productive place to work.

- **Team-working and performance management**. This can cover areas where the insight of a psychologist can provide recommendations on how employees work as a team, and where there may be opportunities for development. Employees may be encouraged to use psychometric tests to gain insight into their own strengths and weaknesses, which can then be worked on using a range of team activities, tasks and coaching and mentoring.

How do I know if this profession is right for me?

As experts in the field of the science of work, many employers will be looking to recent graduates to set an example for others to follow in the areas of communication, business acumen and professionalism. Furthermore, as a consultant, you will also be required to 'sell' your skills and recommendations to clients, managers and staff who may be sceptical or resistant to what you are suggesting.

Consequently, you will need to be credible, persuasive, resilient, with a positive 'can do' attitude and a genuine interest in people and how they function as individuals and in groups. You can gain additional credibility and respect from your organisation by demonstrating good business acumen with a focus on cost-saving or revenue generation, evidence-based recommendations, and people skills that help you to build networks and relate to all people at all levels of seniority. You will also need to demonstrate a high level of competence in psychometrics or statistical analysis, and be able to work under pressure and cope with deadlines. Arguably, as a psychologist you should be at an advantage over others because you can use your experience in understanding yourself and other people to great effect.

'What I really get a kick out of in my job is the thing that others find difficult – the human bit. Employers are constantly looking for leaders who can demonstrate soft skills - i.e. those qualities that reveal a mastery of the sophisticated relationships and dynamics between humans in the workplace - and for me as a business psychologist, this is where I can really add value: to lead by example, inspire and bring about significant change to an organisation and its people .'

What is the progression path to become an occupational psychologist?

Careers and qualifications

In the field of occupational psychology there are two standards necessary for professional practice:

1. Being legally entitled to use the title 'occupational psychologist' and professionally recognised

2. Being professionally entitled to use the title 'chartered psychologist'

Title	Occupational psychologist	Chartered psychologist
Title status	Legally recognised	Professionally recognised
Awarding body	Health and Care Professions Council	British Psychological Society
Types	Registered occupational psychologists can also use the titles **registered psychologist or practitioner psychologist**	Chartered psychologists work in different areas of psychology. Those working in the field of occupational psychology are **Members of the Division of Occupational Psychology**. The types of Division Membership for Chartered Psychologists are: • Full member • In training member • General member

Table 10.1: Title characteristics of occupational and chartered psychologist statuses (Adapted from BPS, 2012)

What stages are involved in the application process?

We have touched on this in previous chapters, but in further detail there are three stages involved in becoming fully qualified to register as a chartered psychologist with the British Psychological Society (BPS) and the Health and Care Professions Council (HCPC).

Stage 1. This requires you to have GBC with the BPS (see Chapter 2).

Stage 2. To qualify for admission to a BPS master's recognised course you must have already gained a first degree in psychology. There are currently 16 universities offering BPS-accredited courses, available as full-time options to be completed in one year, or part-time over two or three years. Some work experience is useful, particularly in the fields of human resources or business management, as many universities will be expecting you to show during the interview how the main areas of study in occupational psychology can be applied to work.

On this basis, it is highly recommended that you look at the BPS curriculum for master's courses, and think about how your work experience maps onto these areas.

Top tip

Master's courses require you to carry out desk and field research which includes the design and development of questionnaires and interviews, critical analysis of text and data, and the use of statistical software packages such as SPSS. It is also assumed that you will be competent in the use of computers and desktop software such as Microsoft Outlook, Word, Excel and PowerPoint. Many full-time courses will expect you to attend university lectures for two to three days a week, with the rest of your time taken up in distance learning over the internet, and / or research.

As a result, you will also need to manage your time, your workload, your resources and your relationships well as you will be working hard for a full year. As a result of this commitment, you should find the course stimulating, challenging and enjoyable and the best foundation to become an occupational psychologist in training who respects the value of evidence-based recommendations, and the importance of working ethically in respect of the BPS principles and guidelines.

Stage 3. On completion of an accredited master's degree, you can train to become fully qualified to register as a chartered psychologist with the British Psychological Society and with the Health and Care Professions Council. This requires a further two or three years of relevant work experience, under the supervision of a chartered occupational psychologist, which demonstrates breadth of practical application skills in five of the eight areas, and in-depth work with clients in one of the four fields of:

*   Work and the environment
*   The individual
*   The organisation
*   Training

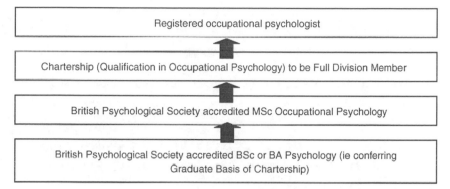

Figure 10.1: The route to becoming an occupational psychologist (Adapted from the British Psychological Society, 2012)

To work as an occupational psychologist (OP) in most companies you will initially need to demonstrate that you have qualified as an OP on a BPS accredited Master's course in Occupational Psychology and achieved chartership status and legal recognition by the HCPC. You cannot call yourself an occupational psychologist until you have achieved this. The BPS has recently launched a revised process for accreditation. More details can be found on the BPS website.

People working towards either the legal or the professional title can be called 'occupational psychologists-in-training' or 'trainee-occupational psychologists', but are not allowed to call themselves 'occupational psychologists'.

How is the occupational psychology course structured?

Work psychology modules focus on four areas of learning including: development of knowledge and understanding, intellectual skill development, practical skill development and transferable skill development.

All British Psychological Society accredited MSc Occupational Psychology Master's degree courses cover eight knowledge areas:

1. Human-machine interaction
2. Design of work environments
3. Personnel selection and assessment
4. Performance appraisal and career development
5. Counselling and personal development
6. HRD and training
7. Employee relations and motivation
8. Organisational development and change

Consequently as a master's student you will need to be comfortable with group working, utilisation of learning resources, self-evaluation, information management, independent study, communication and problem-solving.

What are the differences between courses in terms of structures, content, focus and accreditation bodies?

All courses will expect a 3,000-word literature review for each of the eight of the BPS knowledge areas. This document will enable you to expand upon your opinion on the knowledge area, and back up your argument with research. Some courses, for example London Metropolitan University's MSc in Occupational Psychology, also ask for an accompanying 3,000 word client report for each module. Although this will require you to do more work, it is excellent preparation in terms of research, client liaison, report writing and presentation, for what you can expect when you begin work for a company. You will also be asked to write a 9,000 word dissertation at the end of the course.

Due to the requirement for work experience and a postgraduate qualification, a lot of entrants to occupational psychology are mature students over 25, who may have had a career break, but who will also have relevant work experience. However, it could be argued that a good course will have a mix of students from all ages and backgrounds, so that it reflects the diverse nature of work in the world today, and provides a forum where all students can learn from different perspectives. Whatever the course, you should find one that meets your practical, academic and professional needs; once embarked on the course, a lot will be expected of you and it is important you can focus on doing your best.

How much will it cost?

A three-year full-time BSc in Psychology will cost UK and EU students on average £7,000 (£4,000 part-time), with international students paying on average £10,000 (£5,000 part-time). During this time, some students find that they are able to hold down part-time jobs in order to pay their way through university, although this should always be carefully considered, so that you do not end up compromising your study time.

If you are a full-time UK student you can apply to Student Finance England for a loan to cover your fees, a loan to help with your living costs, and to see if you are eligible for a grant to help with your living costs. Some universities also offer loans for some full-time students whose families are on low incomes. If you are a UK student intending to study part-time you can apply for a loan to cover the cost of your tuition fees. If you have studied at degree level before, or have a previous degree you may not be eligible for a loan, and will have to fund your own studies for the duration of the course.

Average fees for a one-year full-time or part-time master's course are about £7,000 for UK and EU students. International students will pay about £12,000. However, due to the demands of the course, it is unlikely that you will have the time to hold down a job, so you will need to factor in your cost of living without earning for a year. Many universities now offer a January and September intake.

What careers can I enter into with my qualification?

Occupational psychology is an exciting and developing profession. As more businesses look to gain competitive advantage in a fast moving and global business climate, many of them are looking at getting the most from their people in order to achieve this.

An occupational psychologist is ideally placed to offer evidence-based recommendations to help an organisation get results. However, there is very stiff competition from business 'gurus', motivational speakers, trainers and other 'so called' professionals who do not have the same training in evidence-based research as occupational psychologists do, but who are better at marketing and promoting themselves to potential clients looking for a solution.

Typical employers tend to be larger private or public sector organisations where there is sufficient number of staff to merit a human resource development or management function. Many occupational psychologists work for consultancies which have a small number of staff, and which may specialise in areas such as leadership development, recruitment and selection, psychometric testing and coaching.

Some occupational psychologists are self-employed, where they may offer a blend of developmental, research and consultancy work for privately-sourced clients or third party services such as employee assistance programmes or training companies, while others have moved into academia, where they fulfil teaching roles and consultancy services.

Jobs may be advertised in:

- BPS Job Board (Division of Occupational Psychology)
- Chartered Institute of Personnel and Development website
- *Personnel Today* magazine
- Civil Service Jobs online
- Various HR magazines – *HR Today*, *People Management* etc.

Top tips

Many graduates start out by accepting internships where they can build their interpersonal skills and get an understanding of how occupational psychology fits into the world of work.

In a competitive job market, the more work experience you can demonstrate, the better. It is highly recommended that you sit down with a lecturer, or an experienced OP, and go through your CV, rewording and reworking it so that it uses the language and terminology that appeals to prospective employers, the company you want to work for, and the industry you want to work in. As an occupational psychologist, you would be well advised to learn the principles of marketing and sales, to analyse your target market, refine your product and price, and develop yourself as a brand. This will help you to be more focused and persuasive when it comes to fielding questions from prospective employers.

Top tip

Many students make the mistake of over-emphasising their academic qualifications, when in fact, most employers will be looking to see how you have understood the principles of occupational psychology in the work experience you have gained, and applied them to create change in the workplace. Remember to flag up your achievements – convert your experience into a benefit for the company in terms of saving costs / time / effort or generating revenue / time / resource.

Some graduates are disappointed that the area that they are working in as an occupational psychologist turns out not to be to their liking, but it is worth adopting a scientific view of the experience.

Remember that no job is entirely bad: analyse it for pros and cons, always remembering how you are going to work this into your CV, and then think of how you are developing yourself as a distinctive 'brand' for sale within a competitive jobs market. It is always easier to get a job within a company you are already working in than from outside, so focus on building relationships.

Top tip

Attempt to change the situation at work by building relationships, alliances and connections within your department and throughout the company; read the trade press to stay up to date on key themes and developments so that you can impress prospective employers with your knowledge; go to as many trade fairs (CIPD / HR / BPS / health and safety / employee benefits) and networking events as you can; seek out relevant free/paid for training, contribute to blogs and wikis to build an online presence and volunteer to sit on a BPS working group or panel.

Once you have established yourself in a role, there are many opportunities to work your way up in organisations in the fields of HR, recruitment, executive search, development, training, coaching, or change management. Large consultancy firms will take graduates on a salary of £25,000 to £30,000, with an expectation that you will be fast-tracked through a series of graduate development initiatives. You can then expect to be on a salary of £50,000 at consultant level after ten years, and £70,000 to £100,000 as a senior consultant.

Remember that occupational psychology fits into all areas of work, and therefore as a profession, may be less restricted to finding employment in big cities than others, and although it may take time to find a role that allows you to develop your skill set, there is an opening for you somewhere. It may take persistence, effort and time but the rewards are great, and you will be contributing to an increasingly important and highly regarded community of psychologists who are driven to improve the lives of others at work and in society.

Chapter summary

Arguably, work is what changes us more than any other influence. Besides it being a daily necessity, our work also defines, motivates, challenges, frustrates and fulfils us during the estimated 10,000 hours that we spend at it over a lifetime. Increasingly, organisations are waking up to the idea that if they are to retain any competitive advantage in the fast-moving global market, one of the few ways they can differentiate themselves from their competitors is through the unique talents of their people. The ascendancy of strategic human resource management and the current obsessions with engagement, change management and social / psychological capital reflects this desire for companies to retain and get more out of their staff.

Companies are also expected to consider ethical practice and be more accountable to their customers, shareholders and employees who are using technology to track and comment on a company's performance. As such, many companies regard their employees as customers now, and need to be seen to be treating them with the same concern for their welfare and opinion. In a fluid, dynamic and global job market, and with employees' expectations of their psychological contract, employees can vote with their feet if their expectations are not met.

Consequently, the role of the occupational psychologist has become steadily valued over time from companies looking to bring some evidence-based rigor to the challenges of people management. The market is saturated with business people who appropriate the findings that come from occupational psychology research, and who go on to apply it without understanding the value and limitations of the science used to generate it. If you can combine the best of business with the best of occupational psychology, then you really will have competitive edge.

Occupational psychology makes for a fascinating profession and rewarding career. In some ways, it is easier to enter than other professions in psychology: even those who may not have studied at practitioner level, can draw on their work experience and enter into related fields of HR, learning and development, management and marketing from which to analyse from a psychological perspective. This can be a great way to identify which field of occupational psychology to specialise in, and perhaps more importantly, gain insight into the business, organisational and commercial imperatives that drive modern day companies.

One criticism of occupational psychologists is that some of them don't understand how to talk to the client: that they come over as being 'too scientific'. This may be attributable to the relatively low profile of occupational psychology as a profession, and that most people don't understand what they do, and so jump to conclusions. The other point of view is that occupational psychologists don't speak the client's language, and don't empathise with the factors affecting business, knowing when to emphasise the value of evidence-based research – and when not to.

Key points

- As you enter into the field of work, use any job role to develop your profile as a business person who understands the challenges and opportunities that companies face today, and who can 'talk their language'.

- Think of yourself as a scientist, who understands how critical thinking, analysis, and evidence-based research gained from the field of occupational psychology can add value to an organisation. This will make your work more interesting, set you apart from your colleagues and improve your career prospects.

Useful resources

The website for the BPS Division of Occupational Psychology is a huge resource for research, contact information and details on how to qualify and charter as an occupational psychologist: http://dop.bps.org.uk

The *Occupational Digest* provides engaging, authoritative reports on the latest psychology research papers. The editor trawls hundreds of peer-reviewed journals looking for the latest findings from across the breadth of psychological science: www.bps-occupational-digest.blogspot.co.uk

EU and international students can find more details about funding from www.gov.uk/browse/education/student-finance

The following websites advertise jobs in occupational psychology.

BPS Jobs Board:
http://dop.bps.org.uk/dop/organisations/job-board/job-board_home.cfm

CIPD website:
www.cipd.co.uk/

Personnel Today magazine:
www.personneltoday.com/Home/

Civil Services Jobs online:
https://jobsstatic.civilservice.gov.uk/csjobs.html/

HR magazines: *HR Today*, *People Management* etc:
www.peoplemanagement.co.uk/pm/

References

The British Psychological Society (2012) *Occupational psychology* [Online] Available at: //www.bps.org.uk/careers-education-training/society-qualifications/occupational-psychology/occupational-psychology [Accessed 07 December 2012].

The British Psychological Society (2012) *Careers and qualifications* [Online] Available at: http://dop.bps.org.uk/dop/psychologists/standards-development/careers-qualifications/careers-qualifications_home.cfm [Accessed 7 December 2012]

Chapter 11

Becoming
a forensic
psychologist

Dr Gareth Norris

What is forensic psychology?

The role of the forensic psychologist is as broad as it is fascinating. A plethora of crime dramas (such as *Cracker*) and high-profile cases (for example, the murder of Rachel Nickell) in the 1990s brought the field to the forefront of public interest. A natural progression was the demand for academic courses to support this growing awareness of the work of forensic psychologists. However, as with many portrayals gleaned from the entertainment media, the dramatised roles were vastly different than those performed by their real life counterparts. Nevertheless, forensic psychology is increasingly one of the most consistent recruitment options for undergraduate and postgraduate study.

Top tip

The term 'forensic' can be defined as pertaining to the courts and / or the law more generally.

In a relatively early assessment of the field, Blackburn (1993) suggests that the term 'forensic' relates specifically to 'a legal forum, ie a judicial body or court'. Notwithstanding its brevity, such a definition is perhaps too restrictive to fully encompass the diversity in modern forensic psychology practice; consider, for example, the psychologist who provides rehabilitation programmes in prison or the specialist who may advise police during hostage negotiations. Davies, Beach and Hollin (2012) propose that forensic psychology actually, 'embrace[s] both legal and criminological research and application ... a variety of studies at the interface of psychology and the law, spanning both legal and criminological issues...' Hence, we can see that the term 'forensic' is not definitive in the sense that it outlines or relates to any one particular career path or theoretical body of knowledge.

So it would appear that there is some discrepancy over whether the term 'forensic' is related specifically to the courts / law or whether it has a wider application to the study of investigations and understanding criminal behaviour / treatment also. Indeed, in support of this dichotomy Davies *et al* cite the renaming of the Division of Legal and Criminological Society to the Division of Forensic Psychology by the British Psychological Society (BPS) in 1999.

BPP
LEARNING MEDIA

Top tip

Criminological and legal psychology: the former embraces ideas of the antecedents of criminal behaviour (eg mental illness), whereas the latter focuses more on the way psychology can inform the process of legal proceedings (eg eyewitness testimony; see Davies, Hollin and Bull, 2008).

What do forensic psychologists do?

'People always ask me, "Why do people become criminals?" The real answer is that there are a number of different "paths" into offending behaviour. It is my job to untangle some of those and help offenders to lead positive lives on release from prison.' **Forensic Psychologist – HM Prison Service**

At a broad level, Davies *et al* (2012) helpfully divide the field of forensic psychology into four key areas:

1. The causes of crime
2. The detection of crime
3. Legal processes
4. Risk assessment and treatment of offenders

It is here that we can begin to explore the various roles and responsibilities that forensic psychologists may fulfil in the various institutions which secure their services. Davies *et al* (2012) outline a range of these roles within forensic psychology, including:

• Piloting and implementing treatment programmes with offenders

• Undertaking assessments of risk for violent and sexual offenders

• Writing reports and giving evidence in court

• Advising parole boards and mental health tribunals

• Advising on interview techniques with suspects and vulnerable witnesses

This is by no means an exhaustive list! Depending upon the path you hope to follow and the opportunities that arise, you could find yourself working in one or more of these posts.

BPP
LEARNING MEDIA

Is it like they show on TV?

Possibly more so than any other branch of psychology, it might be useful at this point in the discussion to explain what forensic psychology *is not*! Many prospective students will have garnered an interest in this field from watching popular television dramas and Hollywood adaptations of infamous cases and fictional accounts. One of the first was *The Silence of the Lambs*. The main premise of the story is to 'profile' the unknown killer based upon Hannibal Lecter's knowledge of past cases and an FBI agent's training in behavioural evidence. The screen version spawned a huge interest in this genre of film, its appeal lying in the expertise of the 'outsider' rather than the more traditional detective led dramas. However it should be pointed out that neither character is a forensic psychologist!

Top tip

What a forensic psychologist is not!

- Crime scene investigator (CSI)
- Forensic scientist
- Police detective
- Forensic psychiatrist
- Offender profiler (although some 'profilers' can be forensic psychologists)
- A psychic!

Another more recent area of popular media that has fostered a great interest in crime and its investigation is US television series such as *Crime Scene Investigation (CSI)* and *Law and Order*. However, not only do the roles depicted in these dramas not accurately portray the work of a *forensic scientist*, they are most *definitely not* representative of *forensic psychology*. True, there is a certain level of theorising over motivation and offender characteristics, but these roles are very often amalgamated to fit around a fast moving script with limited actors. Forensic scientists will usually have completed a degree in physics, chemistry or biology before dedicated postgraduate (PG) training in forensics accompanied by applied vocational experience in specific areas (eg DNA analysis). As we will see, forensic psychology is also a highly specialised field; even within the wider divisions (investigation, court, corrections etc), there are further niche areas (eg treatment of sexual offenders). Hence, any individual who could demonstrate a high level of competency in these domains would unlikely to also be a forensic science expert also! These positions – while both valuable to the detection, investigation and prosecution or crime – are completely different beasts.

There are one or two other roles that are very similar to forensic psychology, but have some subtle differences. The first is forensic *psychiatry*. Very often the two labels (psychiatry and psychology) are used interchangeably, and, indeed, the two professions might even perform the same role (for example, providing evaluations of offenders at court). However, the distinction lies in the training of the two, with the former holding a medical degree alongside a period of training in psychiatry (known as a *residency*). Alongside the differences in training is the fact that as a medical doctor, the psychiatrist is legally permitted to prescribe medication whereas generally a psychologist is not. This highlights the key difference between the two theoretically; psychiatry focuses more on the medical model whereas psychology possesses a cognitive and behavioural approach. Although the behaviours they examine might be the same (or even the same person!), the conclusions they reach over the antecedent and treatment may be quite dissimilar.

Top tip

What's the difference?

- Forensic psychology: a branch of applied psychology mostly related to the work of the courts, police and prisons

- Forensic psychiatry: a sub-section of medicine that deals primarily with disorders of the brain – can also work with courts, police and prisons, as well as healthcare settings

- Investigative psychology: technically a sub-discipline of forensic / applied psychology that is particularly focused on the work of the police (eg interviewing, behavioural advice or 'profiling', detecting deception, and so on)

The other role related to forensic psychology worthy of mention here – particularly for students seeking to undertake postgraduate study – is the field of *investigative psychology* (IP). Developed from the work of David Canter and his colleagues, the field grew out of his involvement in a number of high profile cases and has grown to encompass a range of topics, from interviewing techniques to understanding terrorism.

Is a career in forensic psychology right for me?

'Working with offenders can challenge your perception of human nature. However, the training and professional support provide you with the ability and strength to remain objective.' **Trainee Forensic Psychologist – voluntary drug rehabilitation centre**

Certainly, a career as a forensic psychologist is intellectually challenging and contains some intrinsic fascination that will undoubtedly maintain your interest for many years! However, this is a challenging role, both in respects of the training required and the more general day-to-day material you may be required to deal with. While it may be interesting to learn about criminal behaviour in the classroom, it is a far cry from having to deal with many critical incidents that could arise.

Let us begin with the positives – putting the title 'forensic' before anything appears to give it a certain kudos, for example, consider 'forensic accountant' or 'forensic odontology' (dentist). Not limited to the portrayal of the role of the behavioural expert in crime dramas, forensic psychology is a field which has a high level of recognition and admiration. However, for those serious enough to go through the training, there needs to be more motivation than this (see the section below *How to qualify...* for more detail). Similarly, despite the level of education and training involved, the salary for forensic psychologists doesn't quite compare with their medical counterparts. As a rough guide, you could expect to earn about £20,000–25,000 a year as a trainee or newly qualified psychologist. Fully qualified forensic psychologists may earn around £30,000–45,000 and consultants / heads of departments may earn up to £65,000–85,000 depending upon the sector.

Some of the key skills you may need include:

*   A genuine desire to help offenders – many people are interested in learning about 'why' people commit crime; however, the forensic psychologist needs to *apply* this knowledge to the individual's circumstances.

*   High levels of patience, empathy, honesty and integrity – many of the people you encounter will have come from challenging environments and you will need to be willing to consider their backgrounds and needs to have a positive impact upon their lives.

*   Good team-working skills – forensic psychologists increasingly work within multi-disciplinary teams and you will need to be able to converse with people from within and external to your profession and organisation.

- A high level of communication skill, both written and verbal – competent record keeping and the ability to communicate your opinions are vital to the practice of forensic psychology, for example, providing written or verbal testimony to a court.

- Good problem-solving and decision making skills – no two cases or individuals will be the same and the forensic psychologist needs to develop practical skills to deal with challenging and fast-changing environments.

- Research skills and the ability to analyse and present statistical data – forensic psychology is a growing field and you will need to keep up-to-date with recent research and also conduct your own investigations on occasion.

Stress is a key factor affecting professionals employed in forensic settings. As a forensic psychologist you will need to develop a range of coping strategies in order to deal effectively with the demands of the field. Good working relationships with your colleagues and particularly more senior psychologists in a 'mentor' role are vital to ensure both a fruitful career and your own psychological health.

Additionally, the training as a forensic psychologist doesn't end with securing your chartership. Certainly, there are formal requirements to complete specific hours of targeted continued professional development (CPD). Alongside formal commitments for progression and advancement is an obligation to keep up-to-date with developments in the field. Research is published in peer reviewed journals, for example, the Division of Forensic Psychology's own publication, *Legal and Criminological Psychology*, contains major developments in the wider field. Targeted journals and books also disseminate research findings and good practice to specific roles within forensic practice, for example, *Psychology in Prisons* (Crighton and Towl, 2008). Presentation at conferences, such as the BPS Annual Conference and / or divisional proceedings, should also be pursued.

Top tip

The prospective forensic psychologist should be aware that their 'education' is a continuing process and be willing to undertake additional study throughout their career.

How to qualify as a forensic psychologist – deciding upon undergraduate and postgraduate study

With so many undergraduate courses available under the forensic-criminological heading, it is no wonder you may be confused as to where to start! The most important starting point is – obviously – an undergraduate degree in psychology. Ideally, this initial study would be from a BPS accredited provider. The majority of UK university psychology departments have gone through this rigorous validation programme; this ensures that they not only cover specific areas of study (eg research methods, social psychology, and so on), but also that the standard of staff / teaching is of the appropriate standard and facilities (eg lab equipment for experiments) also meets the set requirements.

Top tip

Always check the accreditation status of a course before signing up! You can access a list of BPS accredited undergraduate degrees in psychology by using links given at the end of this chapter.

The content of the undergraduate psychology degree is partly prescribed by the BPS, but many will also offer a range of different modules that often reflect staff / departmental research interests. Undergraduate degrees with an emphasis upon forensic / legal / criminological psychology are relatively new. Certainly before the new millennium there were no real options available to those wanting to focus on this branch of psychology at undergraduate level; instead many students would pursue joint honours programmes in combination with wider social science disciplines, such as criminology or policing. Lies (1992) analysed a number of 'psychology and law' courses in the US and reported a wide spectrum of subject matter covered. Many students are attracted to these courses, when in reality they may have little bearing upon the later opportunities to train as forensic psychologists. A good single honours degree from a BPS accredited department is the only real requirement to gain graduate recognition; indeed it is possible to undertake 'forensic' research in any psychology degree, for example, a dissertation on eyewitness testimony.

However, should you find that you have not enrolled upon or completed an accredited programme, all is not lost as you can look into taking a 'conversion course' (see Useful resources at end of this chapter for specific details on conversion courses). Usually, this is a one-year course for students who have completed a non-accredited psychology degree (or similar) and completion then allows eligibility for Graduate

Basis for Chartered Membership with the BPS. You should be careful that, whatever degree you take, it allows you either direct eligibility or the prospect of conversion. With so many options available – many of which have psychology in the title – it is imperative that your course is in fact going to lead to graduate membership of the BPS.

Whichever route you take (direct or conversion), the completion of an undergraduate programme is only the start on your route to becoming a *chartered forensic psychologist*. Stage 1 of the formal qualification usually involves a BPS accredited MSc in Forensic Psychology (BPS, 2011). Again, as with many undergraduate degrees with forensic / criminological in their title, you must ensure that this is accredited with the BPS as without this the qualification is not suitable to fulfil the requirements of stage 1. Again, you can check this on the BPS website listed at the end of this chapter.

While the BPS accredited postgraduate courses all count towards stage 1 of your training, you will probably find some large differences in the emphasis of these programmes. Some may be biased towards the assessment and rehabilitation of offenders, whereas others contain a more investigative element. There may be a specific reason why you wish to consider a particular course that aligns with your later interests, but in reality they all aim to cover a core range of material and competencies. Subsequently, deciding upon one particular scheme will not necessarily preclude you from entering the profession at any of its different incarnations.

Postgraduate training in forensic psychology:	
Stage 1	Stage 2
• BPS Accredited MSc in Forensic/Criminological Psychology	• Supervised practice (by chartered forensic psychologist)
• One year (F/T), two years (P/T)	• Two years (F/T), four years (P/T)

Table 11.1: Overview of postgraduate training in forensic psychology

Stage 2 of 'Qualifying as a forensic psychologist' steps into the practical aspects of this field and it is here that the training becomes more defined and a range of 'Core Roles' is identified (BPS, 2011):

1.   Core Role 1: Conducting applications and interventions
2.   Core Role 2: Research

3.   Core Role 3: Communicating with other professionals
4.   Core Role 4: Training other professionals

Each of these Core Roles must be accompanied by a separate portfolio of evidence, which includes examples of these roles being conducted by the trainee, a practice diary, a competence log book, and a range of supporting evidence. This period of training – usually two years full-time (or equivalent) – must also be conducted under the supervision of a chartered forensic psychologist.

Case study

Annabel graduated from a London university with a 2:1 joint honours degree in Psychology and Sociology. The psychology element of her degree was accredited by the BPS, so she was able to apply to study on an MSc in Forensic Psychology in the North-west of England. During some research for her dissertation, she shadowed some of the team in the Psychological Services section at a nearby prison. Following her graduation from the master's, Annabel went to work as a trainee forensic psychologist at the same institution and was supervised by the head of psychology there (himself a chartered forensic psychologist). Annabel undertook a number of roles, including joint delivery of the Anger Management programme and providing group therapy to drug users. In addition, she also delivered some lectures at a local university to their MSc Criminological Psychology students in order to satisfy the requirements of her portfolio. After two years, Annabel became a chartered forensic psychologist and has subsequently gone to work in a regional secure unit with forensic mental health patients.

Alternatively, many providers are now combining the stage 1 and 2 training and packaging this academic / vocational practice into a Doctorate in Forensic Psychology. In essence, this does nothing but formally combine the stages into a three-year programme, but also arranges supervision and practice. The additional requirement here is the thesis submitted at the end of the course which converts the training into the doctoral level qualification. However, for practice of forensic psychology there is little to really separate the two 'routes'. Additionally, if you have completed an accredited MSc in forensic / investigative / criminological psychology, some providers allow a 'fast-track' option which incorporates the final two years of supervised practice only (stage 2). This might be particularly attractive to those working in a forensic setting which may be suitable to fulfil these requirements.

Costs and fees

There are obviously a range of costs associated with training in forensic psychology. Alongside the undergraduate degree (three years full-time at £9,000 per annum at a UK university), a recognised MSc will range from £4,000–6,000 (possibly due to change following the undergraduate fee rises). All of these fees assume you are a UK resident and you should check your status with a provider beforehand (many overseas and even EU students may pay substantially more). Additionally, there are potentially costs associated with the stage 2 training dependent upon where and how you secure your placement / work experience. For those lucky enough to secure paid employment in a relevant area the main costs are associated with the assessment and submission of your portfolio (please see the BPS website listed at the end of this chapter).

One final word in relation to becoming a chartered forensic psychologist concerns registration with the Health and Care Professions Council (HCPC). In 2009, a number of professions and their associated titles became protected by law. Essentially, this meant that only people who had successfully completed recognised training (ie stages 1 and 2) were eligible to use these protected titles, of which *forensic psychologist* was one. In practice, the BPS has overall decision-making for defining the standards of this profession, but in order to call yourself a 'forensic psychologist' you must also be registered with the HCPC (for more details see the HCPC website at the end of this chapter).

Working with the police

Of all the functions and environments in which the investigative (and forensic) psychologist may find themselves working, the interest is somewhat overshadowed by the relative fascination over one specific role – *offender profiling*. This is possibly the area admissions tutors are most often asked about by prospective students. We have briefly discussed the disparity between the reality and the dramatised role in the media, but the field is worthy of specific mention for those considering venturing into this area.

In essence, offender profiling (or crime scene profiling / analysis, behavioural profiling, criminal personality profiling, or just profiling) involves the analysis of crime scene behaviours in order to produce a composite sketch of the likely offender. Immortalised in a myriad of Hollywood movies and memoirs of leading investigators, the field was to receive some negative publicity following a number of high profile failings in the use of forensic psychologists in particular (for example, the Colin Stagg / Paul Britton case following the murder of Rachel Nickell).

Case study

Dennis graduated with a first class honours BSc in Psychology and Social Care from a Scottish university. As this degree wasn't accredited by the BPS, he undertook a year-long conversion course at a university in the Midlands before commencing on their MSc in Criminological Psychology and Investigation programme. Dennis had always wanted to work for the police, so upon graduation he moved to London to work as a Community Safety Officer. After two years in this role, he applied for a post as an 'Intelligence Analyst' within the Metropolitan Police. Based at New Scotland Yard, Dennis provides tactical and operational support to major inquiries and was recently a senior advisor to the Olympic Safety and Security Programme.

The good news for those still interested in this field of study and potential employment is that following these problems, a number of attempts were made to standardise the field and opportunities do exist for this type of role, including:

- Behavioural Investigative Advisor (BIA) – a number of police forces and related security services (eg MI5), employ specialist personnel to support the decision-making during critical and major incidents. Much of the knowledge and skills which are nurtured during in undergraduate psychology degrees (eg data analysis, report writing, etc) are analogous with this role. However, there is no specific requirement for certified forensic psychology study / practice as such.

- Crime / Intelligence Analyst – police forces in the UK and overseas employ a range of civilians to work alongside warranted officers to offer general and targeted advice in relation to crime problems generally and also more specialised operations. As with the BIA role outlined above, this does not necessitate a qualification or accreditation in forensic psychology, but many of the skills gained through postgraduate study in this area would undoubtedly be useful;

- Police Detective – in many respects, the budding 'profiler' would be advised to consider the police force itself. In most cases, the role depicted in televised dramas is somewhat a hybrid of the investigating officer and forensic psychologist. Certainly, knowledge of human behaviour is of paramount importance to modern police work and many detectives may pursue postgraduate studies in forensic / investigative psychology.

The above discussion on the definition and history of forensic psychology is unlikely to have provided you with any confidence that the job you hope to pursue in this field even exists! However, the important point to take from the above discussion is that there are a huge range of opportunities for you to explore within the umbrella of forensic psychology. Despite what you may have seen on television, a career in forensic psychology involves more than an 'innate' ability to decipher human behaviour! Those with the determination to complete the training requirements will embark upon a challenging and rewarding career.

Chapter summary

Forensic psychology is a fascinating field with a diverse range of employment opportunities. Many people will gain their basic knowledge from television shows and movies, and – while some are quite accurate – these don't always give the best introduction to this challenging role. Students who are likely to be successful in this field are those who possess an inquisitive and open mind, high levels of personal integrity, and resilience in the face of adversity. The six years of training require a high level of commitment and determination, but the rewards are more than financial; forensic psychologists often work at the cutting edge of applied psychology, including areas as diverse as disaster management, police investigations, providing expert evidence in court and treating dangerous offenders to name but a few. However, the most important thing to take away from this chapter is that you need to make some important choices regarding the study route you take.

Key points

- Forensic psychologists work in a range of environments, including prisons, courts, police, NHS, voluntary organisations and private practice.

- Forensic psychology requires a minimum of six years' training (three years undergraduate, one year taught master's and two years supervised practice).

- Look for BPS accredited courses (undergraduate and master's).

- Conversion courses are available for students with non-accredited undergraduate psychology / psychology-based degrees.

- Forensic Psychology Doctorates are now being offered to cover stage 1 and 2 of chartership.

Useful resources

British Psychological Society (BPS): www.bps.org.uk

(BPS) Division of Forensic Psychology: http://dfp.bps.org.uk/

Health and Care Professionals Council: www.hcpc-uk.org

American Psychology-Law Society (AP-LS – Division 41):
www.ap-ls.org

European Society of Psychology and Law (EAPL): www.eapl.eu

References

Blackburn, R (1993) *The Psychology of Criminal Conduct*.
Chichester: Wiley.

BPS (2011). *Qualification in Forensic Psychology (Stage 2):
Candidate Handbook*. [Online] Available at:
www.bps.org.uk/sites/default/files/documents/qualification_in_
forensic_psychology_stage_2_handbook_revised_jan_2011.pdf
[Accessed 02 July 2012].

Crighton, D and Towl, G (2008) *Psychology in Prisons*. 2nd edition.
Oxford: BPS Blackwell.

Davies, G, Beach, A, and Hollin, C 'Introduction'. In Davies, J and
Beech, A eds. (2012) *Forensic Psychology: Crime, Justice, Law,
Interventions*. 2nd edition. Chichester: Wiley-BPS Blackwell. pp. 1–13.

Davies, G, Hollin, C and Bull, R (2008) *Forensic Psychology*.
Chichester: Wiley.

Liss, M. Psychology and law courses: content and materials.
Law and Human Behaviour 1992; 16: 463–471.

Chapter 12

Becoming an educational psychologist

Dr Dimitra Pachi

The relationship between psychology and education has been changing throughout the course of the last century. In the early 20th century educationists were just applying, or trying to apply, psychological theories to resolve educational problems, even if these theories had not been created or tested within the field of education. When psychologists started conducting research on learning and education, they focused on specialised aspects of education, addressing the learning process in a very compartmentalised way. This phenomenon continued until recently (late 20th century), when research in education was accused of losing the broader picture and being completely disconnected from the classroom reality. In the last ten years, efforts have been made to integrate the two disciplines taking the focus away from their differences and putting it back to their intersectionality: the practical aspects of education, ie problems arising within classrooms, have become the starting point for psychological research and theory development, as well as the field of application of inter-disciplinary psychological perspectives from clinical, social, health and developmental psychology (Woolfson, 2011; Slavin, 2012).

The present chapter has been written from this latest perspective, considering educational psychologists as professionals who have knowledge of and work in close collaboration with professionals from other disciplines than psychology and education, as well as with students and their parents. This chapter explores and clarifies potential confusion not only on what educational psychology is but also on how to become an educational psychologist, as well as the challenges and the prospects ahead, in order to provide an updated and comprehensive guide for those of you who consider following this professional route.

Introduction

What are the routes to educational psychology? In order to answer this question, it is very important first to talk about the existing two-fold integration of the disciplines of psychology and education, which leads to two different career routes. On the one hand there is 'Educational psychology', which consists of the study of ways to enhance learning by tackling psychological problems within the educational context, and on the other hand, there is the 'psychology of education', which consists of the study of psychological theories and research relevant to educational issues. According to the British Psychological Society's (BPS) criteria, only the former route of studies leads to Chartership in Educational Psychology; here is the definition that the Department for Education has adopted from the BPS:

'Educational psychologists work with children and young people from birth to nineteen years, and their families, in a variety of settings including schools and homes, and sometimes as part of multi-agency teams. They have competencies in consultation, assessment, case formulation, and intervention related to children's learning, developmental, behavioural, emotional and mental health needs. Intervention may take place at an organisational level, indirectly through parents and teachers, and / or directly with individuals, groups, and families. Educational Psychologists are also involved in evaluation of interventions, research and project work, management and leadership of teams, and offer training to other professional groups.'

(Department for Education, 2011)

This is the route of studies and employment the present chapter is going to describe and discuss in detail.

Top tip

- Educational psychology is the study of ways to enhance learning by tackling psychological problems within the educational context.

- Psychology of education is the study of psychological theories and research relevant to educational issues.

- You will become a psychologist with a specialisation in education.

What does an educational psychologist do?

As an educational psychologist you can work either in the private sector (private schools, private clinics, independent consultancy) or in the public sector (government agencies, educational institutions and so on), on a regular or on a consultancy basis. You are employed to work with students and teachers in order to enhance the learning experience. You have an expertise in processes of learning (the processes of language development, short-term and long-term memory, knowledge, learning of abstract concepts and conducting mathematical calculations), in identifying and in developing strategies to overcome barriers to effective learning such as developmental and conduct disorders (for example, ADHD, dyslexia, dyscalculia, autism, Asperger's syndrome), psychological problems (anxiety etc) and physical impairments (such as partial or complete lack of hearing, lack of sight, limited or no mobility).

While working with students, you will also employ your knowledge and expertise in working with teaching staff to help them deal with students' particularities and individual needs, as well as with their personal-psychological issues related to their teaching experience. You will provide practical advice both on the structure and organisation of the lesson and the management of the class, as well as on dealing with students on an individual basis.

The activities of an educational psychologist can involve any of the following (Kilby and Simms, 2010):

*   Assess students' learning, emotional and behavioural needs in order to develop strategies that can both address these needs and enhance their learning

*   Work in partnership with professionals from other disciplines ie educationists, teachers, clinical psychologists, language and speech therapists, and GPs to provide an accurate and holistic report on the necessary steps to be taken to address students' needs

*   Develop therapeutic and behaviour management programs

*   Help students on an individual basis both to organise their lessons and homework and to manage their emotions and behaviours concerning issues related to their classmates, teachers or parents; help them address relationship issues which might require a third party's advice and direct or indirect intervention

*   Develop projects for students addressing both the national agenda ie Issues of citizenship, and the school's and students' interests

*   Help teachers with psychological issues such as stress management related to their teaching experience: their everyday dealing with students' variant learning progress, students' problematic behaviour, workload, pressure by the administration and by parents

*   Develop courses for parents, teaching staff and other professionals working closely with students and young people

*   Develop and present interventions, which can help local and national initiatives deal with issues related to the learning and class experience ie how to deal with intellectually diverse classes or how to deal with bullying within the class / school context

*   Conduct primary or secondary research on educational issues

Case study

'Working as an educational psychologist has been a real challenge for me, but also I think...the best career choice I have made in my life. I always wanted to work with children, young people in general, and I always knew I wanted to be in psychology, but I did not know exactly in what domain. When I started enquiring about this career path, it seemed quite difficult and quite a distant target, however, things are not as complicated as they sound....once you get your place in a training institution, then it's pretty much straight forward.

Concerning now the amount and the type of work itself, I would like to emphasise that it is a very varied role. As an educational psychologist you have to work with so many people, people from different disciplines and different work environments, however, what is great is that we all work with the same goal...to make young children's school life as beneficial as possible'. **Melissa, Educational Psychologist**

'In the beginning I was afraid to see an educational psychologist, I didn't know if they were like counsellors, I didn't know what to expect; when I met her I saw that she was very nice and helpful. She helped me organise my reading and she gave me some reading techniques. We also talked about my behaviour in school and why I tend to be alone ... I don't have many friends at school. She was really helpful...' **Petra, 17 years old**

Top tip

Your expertise as an educational psychologist lies in:

- Processes of learning: language development, short-term and long-term memory, knowledge, learning of abstract concepts and conducting mathematical calculations

- Strategies to overcome barriers to effective learning such as developmental disorders, physical impairments and conduct disorders

How to become an educational psychologist

In order to become an educational psychologist and be able to perform the aforementioned tasks, there are specific interests, personality characteristics and qualities that you should have, as well

as professional skills that you should acquire. Primarily, you should have a strong interest in children and young people and have strong interpersonal skills with children, adolescents and adults. You should also be caring, extroverted but have tact and patience. These are fundamental personality characteristics, which will not only facilitate, but will make the everyday exercise of your duties an easier, more pleasant and more fulfilling experience.

Formal training

Apart from the aforementioned personality characteristics, you should also acquire a formal training in order to become a professional educational psychologist. Currently, in England (criteria vary in different countries), a three-year full-time doctorate degree is necessary, which consists of one-year of full-time study and two years of training work as a trainee educational psychologist in a local authority (Teaching Agency, 2012). It is the Department for Education and more specifically, since April 2012, the Teaching Agency which is responsible both for the training and the recruitment of candidates. Every year a specific number of places is released and these are split across different universities (you can find all necessary information on the recruitment process, including exact dates and deadlines, on the website of the Department for Education). Some of the universities, providing training places recently are the University of Nottingham, the University of Newcastle, the University of East London, University College London and the University of Southampton; in 2012, 12 universities are each providing five to 12 training places. Now, if you wonder whether you are too old or too young to apply for one of these positions, you should not worry because there are no age restrictions; what is required is that the candidates are able to demonstrate knowledge of the UK educational system and the application of psychological theories in an educational setting.

Entry requirements

There is no age restriction but there are specific requirements set by the Teaching Agency of the Department for Education when you apply for one of the university places described earlier; these are currently the following:

- You need to have GBC with the BPS (see Chapter 2)

- Demonstrate that you have gained relevant experience of working directly with children within educational, childcare or community settings for a minimum of one to two years (this varies between different universities). Training providers are looking primarily for past *paid* work; however, voluntary work should also be added as

it can enhance the candidate's CV. The types of past experience which will be mainly considered include: work in teaching (such as a classroom assistant or a learning mentor) or as a graduate psychologist (as an assistant educational psychologist).

- Finally, be a resident in the UK at the time of application and be able to work in the UK for the duration of the course (three years) and for at least an additional two years after completing the course (a five-year minimum commitment in total is required).

Funding

In terms of funding, there is a funding scheme which is applicable for most positions provided by the Teaching Agency (there are currently no other funding bodies); however, there are some additional self-funded positions. Self-funded applicants will have to apply directly to the training providing institution, while applicants for funded training places will have to apply directly to the Teaching Agency of the Department for Education. You can apply both for funded and self-funded places. The existing funding scheme includes a bursary for Year 1 and fees for all three years (fees vary across training providers). Currently, the bursary levels are £14,400 outside London and £14,900 inside London, which is tax free and paid by the Department for Education directly to the trainee in monthly instalments. The fees for the training are also paid by the Department for Education directly to the training institutions. In Years 2 and 3, students will be working as trainee educational psychologists in a work placement provider, which can be a local authority or another institution; recently most of the work placement providers have decided to pay a sum of around £15,000 per year as a bursary to Year 2 and Year 3 trainees (Teaching Agency, 2012b).

Training outside of England

For information on becoming an educational psychologist and for training places outside England you can contact the University of Cardiff in Wales, Queen's University Belfast in Northern Ireland and the University of Dundee or the University of Strathclyde in Scotland. According to the Welsh system, a three-year doctorate programme is necessary which is provided only by the University of Cardiff and the programme is only partly funded by the Welsh Assembly, with a £4,000 contribution by each trainee. In the Scottish system, a two-year master's programme is necessary followed by an one-year probationary professional placement as an Associate Educational Psychologist. In Scotland the programmes are fully funded by the Scottish government and the programmes are provided in alternate years by the University of

Strathclyde and the University of Dundee.

Developments in training

In terms of the training provided in England, nation wide research has shown that the current training model is not sustainable in its current form; improvements should be made to specific problematic areas:

1. There should be one consistent centrally managed programme; the three-year project should have a more hollistic approach which together with its centralised management will not bear any uncertainly regarding either procedural or conceptual issues.

2. Changes should be made to the process of finding placements for ccoond and third year students.

3. Changes should be also made to ensure parity with other similar psychology professions.

4. Possibilities should exist for combined applied psychological approaches.

5. The curriculum of the training should keep up to date with the latest research findings in child development and therapeutic strategies. In addition, alternative funding options have to be found as the local authorities face more and more problems in providing funding for the trainees, especially under the current economic situation.

Continued professional development

Despite the problems that current training models have and the confusion caused by the differences between different countries / areas, even within the UK, what is self-regulated and independent is that once you have qualified as an educational psychologist, you should not stop training and learning throughout your career. As research in different disciplines continues to provide us with new information on the conditions and factors affecting learning, which can help us understand in depth the processes which take place both at an individual and group / social level, educational psychologists have a duty to keep up to date with the latest theoretical and empirical findings. Similarly they have to keep up to date with the continuous advances in technology which affect tools used for teaching and learning, as well as for the diagnosis and therapy of developmental disorders related to learning. Short courses, attending relevant academic and non-academic conferences, reading as well as personal research can also help to achieve that goal.

Career prospects

The majority of career opportunities for educational psychologists lie with local educational authorities in nurseries, schools, colleges and special units of education. However, there are also private consultancies, which employ educational psychologists providing services privately to parents and teaching institutions. However, the private sector has been traditionally commissioned by legal services and parents in order to challenge the work / assessment delivered by educational psychologists employed in the public sector, therefore, creating tension between the professionals working in the private and the public sector. Apart from the private sector, nowadays there is also a growing demand for educational psychologists by charities, voluntary organisations and social enterprises.

In the public sector, the professional path you can follow is from an assistant level to a principal educational psychologist level or to other areas of the local council's educational services or children's services department. A guide in 2011–2012 of the different salary ranges, depending on the level of career, is the following: for an assistant educational psychologist the salary range is from £25,000 to £29,000, for an educational psychologist from £30,000 to £40,000 and for principal educational psychologists up to £55,000.

Chapter summary

It is important to consider very carefully whether educational psychology really is the career for you. If you decide to follow this career path you will have to be prepared for hard work as you will be dealing both with young people with special needs but also with adults who are not always ready to accept the recommendations of a non-teaching staff member. However, as an educational psychologist you have the responsibility to help as much as possible both the young people with their learning, psychological and social difficulties, as well as those involved with them (teachers, parents and so on) in the most beneficial way for the young people. The educational psychologist has to see past individual and / or professional ambitions or egos and strive always for the young people's benefit in order to give them the resources to help them proceed with their lives in the best way possible. They have a very important role not only in the educational system but also in society in general.

Key points

- Important personality characteristics are to be caring, extroverted, have tact and patience, strong interest in children and young people and strong interpersonal skills.
- Professional criteria:
  - A three year full time doctorate degree, which consists of one-year of full-time study and two years of training work as a trainee educational psychologist in a local authority
  - The ability to demonstrate knowledge of the UK educational system and
  - The ability to demonstrate knowledge of the application of psychological theories in an educational setting

  There is no age limitations for applicants.
- Requirements for the doctorate degree:
  - A GBC accredited psychology degree or a conversion course
  - Experience of working directly with children within educational, childcare or community settings for a minimum of one to two years and
  - UK residency and work permit at least for five years

- The bursary levels are £14,400 outside London and £14,900 inside London, tax free and paid by the Department for Education directly to the trainee in monthly instalments.
- Career opportunities lie mainly with local educational authorities in nurseries, schools, colleges and special units of education.

Useful resources

For more information on the funding and the application process please refer to www.education.gov.uk/ and the Teaching Agency.

For information on conferences, publications, interest groups and membership criteria please refer to www.bps.org.uk and the Division of Educational and Child Psychology: http://decp.bps.org.uk/.

For information on the salaries and working conditions of professional educational psychologists please refer to www.aep.org.uk/.

References

Department for Education (2012) *Developing Sustainable Arrangements for the Initial Training of Educational Psychologists. Final Report (November 2011)*. [Online] Available at: http://dera.ioe. ac.uk/12355/1/review%20of%20educational%20psychologist%20 training%20final%20report.pdf [Accessed 29 May 2012].

Kilby, C and Simms, M (2010) *Educational Psychologist Job Description* [Online] Graduate Prospects and AGCAS. Available at: www.prospects.ac.uk/educational_psychologist_job_description.htm [Accessed 21 November 2012].

Slavin, R (2012) *Educational Psychology, Theory and Practice*. 10th edition. Boston: Pearson.

Teaching Agency, Department for Education (2012) *Educational Psychology* [Online] Teaching Agency. Available at: www.education. gov.uk/schools/careers/careeropportunities/b00201184/educational-psychology [Accessed 29 May 2012].

Teaching Agency, Department for Education (2012b)*Educational Psychology: Funding* [Online] Teaching Agency. Available at: www.education.gov.uk/schools/careers/ careeropportunities/b00201184/educational-psychology/training/ funding [Accessed 21 November 2012].

Woolfson, LM (2011) *Educational Psychology: The Impact of Psychological Research on Education*. England: Pearson / Prentice Hall.

BPP
LEARNING MEDIA

Chapter 13

Becoming
a research
or academic
psychologist

Dr Emese Csipke

What is a research psychologist?

> **Definition:**
>
> A research psychologist works to discover, uncover and prove new ideas in the broad field of psychology, by adhering to scientific methodology.

A research psychologist is someone whose primary role is to conduct research. Research itself can be defined as the systematic search for knowledge to discover and prove novel ideas, develop theories or solve problems. Its goal is to advance scientific and human knowledge. A researcher will work within the framework of the scientific method. Within psychology this could mean evaluating the efficacy of a new treatment for a specific mental health problem, developing theories about the way humans or animals acquire knowledge or understanding how advertising affects shopping behaviour. The possibilities are nearly limitless. Essentially there is research being conducted in psychology across the broad fields of clinical, cognitive, occupational, educational, health, forensic, personality and many more. Your undergraduate degree will give you some indication of which fields are attractive to you.

What does a research psychologist do?

Research psychologists can be found working in academic settings, the NHS, for governments or charities and even in industry. Where you work will depend on the type of research interests you have. At the beginning of your career your role will usually concentrate on carrying out the day-to-day duties of research. These include running experiments / lab work, recruiting participants for research projects, data collection and maintaining project databases. You can expect to be involved in data analysis and the writing up of reports and articles for publication. Once you have some experience in working on successful research projects, supervisors will expect you to contribute to funding applications, ethics applications, and supervising junior researchers. By this stage your CV should include a list of good quality papers published in peer-reviewed journals (each article you write is sent to others in your field to be assessed for scientific merit). These are attractive to future employers as their funding and prestige are based in part on their academic staff's contribution to science. The phrase 'publish or perish' is often used to describe the push by departments and universities in relation to the need to continually write peer-reviewed papers.

As your experience builds, you will be invited to contribute to your field more broadly. For example you may join your local ethics committee where your expertise is relied upon to judge the ethical merits of fellow scientists' projects. You will most likely be invited to be a reviewer for some peer-reviewed journals and be expected to critique other people's research and judge whether the science is sound and worthwhile enough to publish. This is interesting in itself and also hones your skills when you learn to spot the weaknesses in others' work. As you climb the career ladder you can expect to have a less hands-on role on the day-to-day tasks of research and will typically oversee several research projects / postgraduate students' dissertations and theses quite closely. You will probably also be involved in collaborating with other researchers on national and international trials. You may be invited to join steering groups for other projects, either to give your independent opinion on how another project should proceed, or because you have some specialist knowledge they lack.

Is this right for you?

Interest in research itself, *and* the area you are researching, is vital to be happy in this field. Most people have an area they are primarily interested in, such as clinical psychology or cognitive psychology. Within these broad fields, you can move around as your interests develop and change. Further along in your career you will most likely find that you are working across several projects that are broadly related. For example if your research interest is psychosis you may work on projects looking at social deprivation and its impact on schizophrenia, the efficacy of a new therapy on auditory hallucinations and a project on first-episode schizophrenia and pathways into the mental health services. You don't have to 'specialise' in a strict area however, you may find one aspect of some research you undertake leads you in unexpected new directions. Your job will always entail a variety of tasks and roles, and give you the opportunity to work independently as well as in teams. The variability of the tasks and roles you will be expected to fulfil as well as the variety of research projects is one of the advantages of this career in fact; it is not likely you will be bored.

The ability to self motivate and work independently is essential. No one will be looking over your shoulder on a day-to-day basis. If you are the type of person who benefits from close supervision and frequent small milestones this may not be for you. Patience and the ability to problem-solve are vital. Almost every research project will come up against unexpected obstacles no matter how meticulously planned out and you must be able to think quickly and creatively. These obstacles can include the lack of participants willing to take part therefore jeopardising the viability of the study, distressing information relayed to you by participants, a drug having serious adverse effects on participants and so on. You'll need presence of mind and to be willing to take on the responsibility to deal with these issues.

You will find your work is quite flexible in terms of working hours; you won't always be at a desk in an office, and this role will give you the

opportunity to travel to conferences worldwide to present your work. The amount you travel will be partly up to you. Early in your career you might be asked to represent your research team at conferences. As you progress you can ask junior researchers to attend on your behalf or go yourself. Working for a university in particular also provides such tangible benefits as generous holidays, a reasonable pension scheme (which can be taken with you as you move around universities) and average maternity / paternity leave. However as universities come under financial pressure this might change. It is also possible to work part-time, in combination with another job or personal commitments elsewhere. Although it is a relatively well paid career, if a very high salary is high on your list of priorities, this may not be right for you.

One of the major drawbacks you will come across is that posts are normally tied to funding. If you go down the lecturer to professor route you will be expected to bring funding with you. This is a time consuming and often frustrating task as inevitably there will be several good applications for the same funds and competition is fierce and likely to get fiercer. However, once you are in a lectureship post employment is typically stable. If you work on a project-to-project basis you will be relying on others to bring in the funds and appoint you to run the research, in most cases needing to apply for new posts continually. Universities and unions are working on making these fixed contract research posts more permanent, however the reality is that fixed-term contracts do end at some point. However if you have a good relationship with members of your department or supervisors they will look out for you, at the very least telling you of jobs they know are coming up. Likewise, working for a charity where funding goes up and down doesn't provide the best job security.

Top tip

Why be a research psychologist?

- You spend your time solving problems or improving on things for the benefit of others.

- Your career will involve working on a variety of projects, taking on different roles, working with a variety of people – you'll never get bored!

- It gives you the opportunity to work independently and in teams.

- You won't be tied to a desk, and it's a flexible job.

- You'll have the opportunity to travel internationally to present your work to others in your field.

Assess your skills

Being a research psychologist might not be right for you if...

.... You don't have the patience to see long term projects all the way through

....You aren't flexible in your working style – research can be uncertain and is ever changing – you need to think on your feet and adapt

.... You like to see the results of your work immediately

.... You feel you need close supervision

... You aren't interested in the commitment of a PhD – you'll soon reach the career ceiling without one

.....A high salary is important to you

'When I finished my PhD, I was not certain about whether I wanted an academic career or not... however, a position for a Research Assistant came up in the same department where I had completed my PhD; I decided to apply and I got the job. In the beginning I was not sure if I had made the correct choice but when I got into the research process a bit more, I really started enjoying it and I realised that I had the skills to perform really well. It's been three years now that I have been doing research and my confidence has increased. I have also enjoyed all parts of conducting research, from designing the research tools and conducting the fieldwork, to conducting the analysis of the data as well as interpreting it. Conducting research is very productive and very interesting, because you never know what you are going to find...there could be an element of surprise with your findings! Now that the project I have been working on is coming to an end, I am looking forward to applying for my own research grants and becoming a Research Fellow in a University that has expertise in my field of study' **Terence, Research Assistant**

How do I get started?

Getting a good degree (2.1 or higher) in psychology from a British Psychological Society approved course or related social science is essential. It cannot hurt to have your degree from a university with a good reputation as many potential supervisors / admissions teams will be looking for this. Choosing challenging courses, including statistics, is essential. Excelling at any research aspects of your course (for example your final year project) will look impressive on your CV. Try to take an opportunity to collaborate with a professor or graduate student so that you get some research experience that is outside the realm of your required coursework. If you chose to do a degree in an unrelated field, you will need to complete a conversion course. This will broadly cover the subject matter of a first degree in psychology in a shorter timescale. For further information on which courses are BPS accredited please see the end of the chapter.

In order to work as a research psychologist you will need a PhD in most cases, especially if you work in an academic setting. Certainly without one, you will reach a point where you cannot progress any further on the career ladder. Completing a master's is the minimum. Indeed having a master's degree will give you an advantage when applying for PhD programmes due to the competitive nature of getting on PhD courses. However, some PhD courses have master's built into them (see below). Working as a research assistant / worker on someone else's project also looks good on your CV and is probably essential to do before applying for PhD programmes. If you are interested in clinical research, some clinical experience (for example, assistant psychologist) with the population you are interested in can demonstrate your dedication. While you are building your CV with research assistant roles, try to look for a variety of roles so that the number of skills you have increases and you can demonstrate competence in a variety of areas. At this stage, even if you have your heart set on researching a particular topic, it is not necessary or even desirable necessarily to work on a research project that exactly matches your interests. What is more important is that you get a variety of experience; you can focus on your chosen topic at a later stage.

Top tips for getting started!

- Choose challenging undergraduate courses

- Collaborate with a professor or lecturer to get research experience, even if it is not in your primary field of interest

- Volunteer in settings related to your interests (eg, join a research lab, a nursing home, a helpline)

- Try to get experience in as many areas / roles as possible (eg, various client groups, data collection, recruiting research participants) to demonstrate your wide knowledge

- After graduation work as a research assistant in a university

Where should I do a master's / PhD?

There are several things to consider when 'choosing' where to do a further degree. As emphasised in previous chapters, it is important you ensure first that it is an accredited course. You may also wish to consider the potential supervisory pool at a university. Most departments will have expertise in certain research areas, so you should focus on those where the interests match your own.

Top tip

Questions to consider before choosing a course:

- Are there a few researchers you admire / whose work you are interested in that you'd like to work alongside?

- Is location important for you due to family or financial commitments?

- Is the reputation of a university important to you?

- Does that reputation apply to the specific department you want to work with?

- The cost of living in certain areas is higher than in others which is typically not reflected in funding – does this matter?

The application process

Getting onto a master's programme is relatively straightforward. Universities and departments will advertise them on their web pages and in the prospectus where descriptions of the course and the application process is outlined. The majority of master's courses last for a year. Choose a course that has a large research component to enhance your skills. If you have an exceptionally good degree or have research assistant experience, you might want to apply directly for a PhD programme.

PhD programmes are run by departments and each has their own application process. They typically last for four years. This is usually three years of the PhD, plus an initial first year. The first year is spent either completing three three-month lab rotations, or a one-year taught master's course (commonly called a 1+3). If you have no postgraduate experience, you are more likely to get onto a course with an inbuilt master's. However, don't be surprised if your 1+3 programme requires you to complete the master's component of the course even if you already completed one that is not linked to the PhD. On the other hand, to get on a course with lab rotations a postgraduate master's might be beneficial. In these programmes it is often the case that the research project will be designed ahead of time and you will have less input into the direction it takes, and you won't need to write your own proposal. You may join an existing research team and work on an 'add-on' project that will form your research. The programmes with lab rotations typically expect you to develop your own projects following the lab rotations. You can find these programmes on university/departmental websites as well as www. jobs.ac.uk.

There is also the possibility that you can apply for departmental/ university funding to fund your PhD. To achieve this, you will need to put in a detailed application with a specific description of your research interests as well as a research proposal. For this you will need to identify a supervisor who agrees to supervise you and then usually helps you to plan and write the proposal. This potential supervisor can be someone for whom you are already working as a research assistant. Alternatively, you can try to contact particular people who research in the area you want to be in, tell them you would like to work with them and ask if it would be alright to send them some research ideas you already have. It is helpful in these cases to draft a brief research proposal with which you can demonstrate your knowledge, and understanding of the scientific method and ethical considerations. If the supervisor agrees to work with you to secure funding expect your research ideas to change as you work together.

Planning your finances

While working on a master's or PhD the salary is not very generous, around £13,500 to £21,000, most being at the lower end. Bear in mind a course in London might come with the same funding, but the cost of living is significantly higher than elsewhere. You will probably have to live quite frugally during this period. As a research assistant your salary will start at around £23,000 and typically goes up £55,000, depending on your experience. Lectureships start around £29,000 and as a professor you can expect up to £80,000. If you take on additional responsibilities, such as being a the head of a department, you can expect to be compensated for it in addition to the basic salary. Salaries in charities will probably be less generous, and if you plan on working in industry it will vary from sector to sector. Working in the private industry, especially if your research lies in the area of occupational / marketing is probably the most lucrative salary wise.

What career paths are open to a research psychologist?

Typically, post PhD you will start off in a mid-level research level position, or you will have been lucky enough to get a highly competitive post-doctoral fellowship (which is seen as advantageous if you have ambitions to remain in academia and work your way up to being a professor). As you move up the ladder, you can work toward being a lecturer (but you will probably need many good publications and possibly even demonstrate your ability to attract funding before being offered such a post) then progress towards being a professor. You will most likely be required to contribute to some teaching. This may vary from teaching several classes for undergraduates a week to just a few classes a year. Not all departments have responsibilities for teaching undergraduates so if you would prefer fewer teaching hours, such a department might suit you. Alternatively you can manage increasingly larger number of projects or more complex trials, perhaps in a 'research hub' or organisation. If you have no interest in teaching at all, working your way up the funding / research ladder to become a principal investigator (the main person in charge of large research projects) might be your career path. Whichever research path you go down, or topic of interest, this is a rewarding and enjoyable career.

Case study

'I wasn't sure what I wanted to do with a degree in psychology – I just sort of fell into it. Abnormal psychology appealed to me the most, so initially I thought about pursing a career as a clinician. However, after gaining some research experience and running my own studies, I became more and more interested in research. After finishing my PhD I have worked on a number of research projects always taking on more responsibilities. Not all aspects of it are easy, but overall I'm very glad I chose to go down this road, and wouldn't trade this for a career as a clinician for anything!'

Chapter summary

Being a research psychologist is an exciting and rewarding career choice. It gives you the opportunity to have a job that involves lots of variety – in the research projects you undertake, the different and varied roles you must take on, the tasks your everyday life consists of and more. It is also a flexible role that is unlikely to be solely office based as well as affording you the opportunity to travel. However, in order to get there and achieve once you are there, you must work hard, be self motivated and disciplined.

Key points

- Psychological research occurs in all branches of psychology so there are endless opportunities to find something that matches your interests.

- Research psychologist can work in many settings – academic, healthcare, government, charities or education.

- Working in the field means opportunities to work in teams and independently with a variety of professional disciplines.

- The work is varied, covering teaching, running experiments, interviews and tests with research participants, library work, writing papers and books, and attending conferences.

- Working in a research setting offers a lot of benefits, flexible working and opportunities to make a good salary.

Useful resources

The BPS's online resource for all information relating to accredited courses:
www.bps.org.uk/careers-education-training/accredited-courses-training-programmes/accredited-courses-training-progra

The BPS's online guide to conversion courses:
www.bps.org.uk/bpslegacy/ac

The BPS's information on careers in psychology:
www.bps.org.uk/sites/default/files/documents/your_journey_web.pdf

PhD programmes can be found at: www.jobs.ac.uk
In addition the individual department pages on university websites, as well as the university websites themselves, will have valuable information specific to each university.

Chapter 14

Conclusion

A career in psychology can be very rewarding but also demanding on a personal and professional level. It involves a long training path and commitment to ongoing study throughout your career. Before you decide on whether this is the right career for you, you will need to decide whether you have the skills, interests and personal qualities required.

The first stage towards a career in psychology is to complete a psychology degree. There is a wide variety of courses available and in order to be able to choose the right one, you will need to consider some important factors, such as professional accreditation and employability prospects, as well as more practical and financial issues. If you have completed a non-psychology degree you may still be able to study psychology through the conversion route, by completing a psychology conversion course. This book offers practical advice and tips that can help you through the application and interview process. It also outlines some helpful information that can facilitate your early steps into psychology studies and your first contact with university life.

The financial demands of a degree are very high and psychology is no different in this respect. You will need to plan in advance the cost of your studies and keep within a realistic budget in order to be able to achieve your desired goals. There are grants and discounts available that can help you through this process. A psychology course involves not only theoretical learning but also empirical projects and research. It will equip you with a variety of transferable skills and knowledge that are helpful not only for a career in psychology, but also in different career options – should you decide to change paths.

A comprehensive overview of some of the most popular specialist routes in psychology in the final chapters of this book show that careers in psychology are varied. Therefore, making the relevant provisions or plans from early on in your studies is the best approach in order to maximise your chances of securing a place on these courses. The information provided in the chapters should give you a realistic understanding of the different professions and the requirements that each route may have.

A good piece of advice is to be persistent with your chosen route as it is more often than not the case that it will take you longer to reach your desired destination than anticipated. In order to get there, you must work hard, be self motivated and disciplined. An essential thing to take away from this book is that you need to make some important choices regarding the study route you take. However, becoming a psychologist is very rewarding and makes for a fascinating profession as it gives you the opportunity to play a very important role in shaping our society.

Index

A

Academic psychologist 173
Accredited university courses 17, 66, 87, 118
Applied psychologist 8
Assistant psychologist 102

B

Biological psychology 70
British Psychological Society (BPS) 17, 132
British Psychological Society (BPS) accreditation 17, 66
British Psychological Society (BPS) Chartership 18
British Psychological Society (BPS) membership 56
British Psychological Society (BPS) Qualification in Counselling Psychology 121

C

Careers as a psychologist 81
Clinical psychologist 82, 97, 98
    Application process 104
    Career paths 108
    Finances 107
    Previous experience 102
    Skills required 99
    Training courses 105
Clinical psychology 98
Cognitive psychology 70
Communication skills 6, 10
Compulsory modules 19
Conceptual and historical issues in psychology 70
Continued Professional Development (CPD) 150, 167

Conversion courses 32
Core modules 19, 33, 66, 70
Counselling psychologist 82
    Application process 120
    Career paths 123
    Courses 117
    Finances 122
    Previous experience 119
    Skills required 116
    Training routes 121
Counselling psychology 115
Counselling skills 12
Critical thinking 10

D

Developmental psychology 70
Dissertation 69, 72
Doctorate in Clinical Psychology 82
Doctorate in Counselling Psychology 82, 122
Doctorate in Educational Psychology 83, 165
Doctorate in Forensic Psychology 83, 153
Doctorate in Health Psychology 84

E

Educational psychologist 83, 162
    Activities 163
    Career paths 168
    Finances 166
    Training 165
Educational psychology 161
E-learning 46
Elective modules 19
Employability 22

F

Final year psychology project 69, 72
Forensic psychiatry 148
Forensic psychologist 83, 145
    Career paths 155
    Finances 154
    Postgraduate training 152
    Qualification process 151
    Skills required 149
    Working with the police 154
Forensic psychology 145
Formulation 98
Freshers' week 44

G

Graduate Basis for Chartered Membership (GBC) 17, 67, 101, 132, 165

H

Health and Care Professions Council (HCPC) 18, 87, 132
Health and Care Professions Council (HCPC) registration 18, 81, 101, 117, 154
Health psychologist 84

I

Improving Access to Psychological Therapies (IAPT) 89, 119
Investigative psychology (IP) 148

J

Joint honours course 20

L

Library 46
Listening skills 10

M

Master's in Health Psychology 84
Master's in Occupational Psychology 133
Master's in Sport and Exercise Psychology 85
Mature students 24
MSc in Forensic Psychology 83, 152

N

National Health Service (NHS) 89, 99, 108
Neuropsychologist 84

O

Occupational psychologist 85, 129
    Application process 132
    Career paths 135
    Courses 133
    Finances 135
    Skills required 130
Occupational psychology 129
Open days 23, 37, 43
Open-mindedness 10
Optional modules 19, 73
Organisational psychologist 129

P

Part-time work 59
Patience 9

BPP
LEARNING MEDIA

Pay 8
Personality and individual
  differences 71
Personal tutors 46
PhD programmes 178
Postgraduate funding 59, 87
Postgraduate psychology courses
  86
Professional and Career
  Development Loan 60
Psychology of education 161

Q

Qualities required for psychology
  9

R

Research assistant 102
Research methods and statistics
  71
Research posts 12
Research psychologist 8, 173
  Application process 178
  Career paths 180
  Finances 179
  Skills required 174

S

Sandwich course 21
Scientist practitioners 98
Single honours course 20
Social psychology 72
Specialist areas 73
Sport and exercise psychologist
  85

Student bursaries 58
Student finance 53
Student grants 58, 135
Student loans 57, 135
Students' union 47
Studying psychology 65

T

Teaching 86
Teaching Agency 165
Tuition fees 23, 53

U

Undergraduate curriculum 70
Undergraduate psychology course
  32, 65
Undergraduate psychology course
  structure 65
Universities and Colleges
  Admissions Service (UCAS) 35
University accommodation 23,
  43, 54
University application 31
University application form 35
University facilities 46
University interview 36
University living costs 53
University reputation 22

W

Work experience 11, 90
Working conditions 8